NOT OUT OF THE WOODS

NOT OUT OF THE WOODS

A Year of Agony and Ecstasy in Golf's Foothills

Roger Morgan-Grenville

BIKE SHED BOOKS

Not Out of the Woods

ISBN 978-0-9569176-1-4

First published in 2018 by Bike Shed Books in 2018

© Roger Morgan-Grenville 2018

Cover painting and portrait by Caroline Morgan-Grenville

Typeset, printed and bound in the UK by
Short Run Press Ltd, Exeter, Devon.

CONTENTS

Dedication

To Kate, Sue and particularly Caroline. Who realised and accepted that sometimes men have to do stuff because they just do.

Prologue

BESIDE THE SALT WATER

It was an omen.

A large seagull had shat on the windscreen of my car in the few minutes I had been away from it. Out of all the cars in that smug, salt encrusted half acre, it had chosen mine, and I took it as a sign.

A few minutes earlier, I had been trying to convince the secretary of a near-sanctified Cornish golf course to let my family and I have a round there one evening the following week, and it had not gone well. In fact, it hadn't gone at all.

'Without a handicap certificate, you can't play. Simple as that, I'm afraid.'

I had never seen anyone look less afraid in my life. A giant crocodile in the process of hauling down a wounded wildebeest into the depths of the Mara River would look less afraid than he did. All he had done was make me feel unreasonable for asking the question in the first place.

'But we are fairly experienced golfers. We will respect the course. We won't play slowly. We will call players through if we are holding them up. We will pick up our divots.' It sounded pathetic to me, and must have been doubly so to him.

I was an occasional golfer, C minus at best, but, for some reason, I had wanted to play this course ever since we had first started coming down to Cornwall as a family, two decades ago. When I walked across it each dawn on my way to the beach, there was something rakish about its beauty, as if it was out of an Edwardian period drama. There was something between the dunes and the emerald green grass that drew me inexorably into its orbit. The dead ground beyond each of its alluring contours promised rich, pioneering adventure. The narrowness of its fairways spoke of challenge. The exquisitely manicured greens spoke of heroics. The sun would shine endlessly. The ball would fly in parabolic beauty. My game would be lifted by the environment alone, and I would attain a state of old fashioned sporting grace if only they would give me the chance.

'No handicap, no game,' he said, and started needlessly straightening a small pile of score cards. 'I'm sorry'. He didn't look sorry. He merely looked like the sort of man who unfailingly got his tax return in before the due date each year, and who despised those who didn't. He belonged to that certain class of Briton whose sheer unbending cussedness with rules should entitle their personality to be given the status of a Site of Special Scientific Interest. The interview was clearly over, and all that remained of the exchange was silence.

The drizzle was scudding in horizontally on the sea breeze, and both course and car park were as empty as the Chaplaincy stall at a University Open Day.

It was only when I got back to the car, and saw the contents of the herring gull's recent breakfast on my windscreen that it started to dawn on me that I actually might have more control of this issue than I had assumed. His refusal was for now, not necessarily for ever. Maybe it was even reasonable. He wasn't saying that I could never play there, just that he wanted to see a handicap certificate before he let me do so. All I needed to do was learn the wretched sport properly, attain a handicap, and then present myself to the secretary in a year's time to ask the same question. Then I would brandish my new certificate before him in an insolent manner, claiming my right to give him £75 of my hard-earned money for the privilege of having me swishing around on his precious bloody turf for four hours.

In exactly a year, I promised the gulls, I would be back

here to claim my prize. If it hadn't been for the noise of my engine I might have heard the gulls scream back:

'In your dreams, loser'.

I ignored them, and they went their way, I mine.

Chapter 1

THE UNDERGRADUATE

'Of all the hazards, fear is the worst'
Mac O'Grady

The Undergraduate looked unusually pleased with himself.

'It's what you've been saying for months,' he explained. 'I have to do more in the way of action, and less in the way of talking. So I have, and you should be pleased.'

I examined the leaflet he had brought along with him, and especially the stratospheric costs that had been added in black biro against the blue sky of the beguiling photograph on the front page.

'But look at it!' I said. 'Have they got the decimal point in the wrong place, or something? I mean, that amount would have bought my first two or three cars.'

'But that was back in the 70s and 80s,' he added rather dismissively. 'Things are different now and, anyway, you're always saying that you get what you pay for'.

He looked at his empty pint glass in the way that only a student can, as if idly wondering by what sequence of tiny financial miracles it would come to be full again without worsening his student debt.

Our family had received a small and unexpected inheritance and we had agreed a few evenings before that everyone should come up with ideas for experiences, as opposed to possessions, that we would not otherwise have been able to do, and now could, and that the most compelling one would win. Our doormat, which had never seen a brochure for the Seychelles in its life, suddenly started seeing them raining down like confetti, as it also saw lists of fine wines, skiing holidays and classic rock concerts. There is no enthusiasm like the enthusiasm brought on by a loosening belt.

'The thing about golf,' explained the Undergraduate once the small matter of his thirst had been attended to, 'is that it ticks all the boxes.' He ran through these 'boxes' on the fingers of his right hand. 'One: we can all do it. Two: it's healthy. Three: it's a life skill, and we can get better and better at it. Four: we can use it later on to network.'

I stopped him.

'No one in our family has ever networked, and we

wouldn't know how to. Our hearts wouldn't be in it. It would be like being the Royal Correspondent on the Guardian, always feeling that we were somehow betraying our principles. Besides, we'd be crap at it.'

'And five,' he said, ignoring me completely, 'we could get handicaps and travel round the world playing on beautiful courses, sharing beer, and having quality family time.'

This last comment was a palpable hit, as he knew it would be. He was playing on that parental dread of university aged children getting bored of home and heading off in semi-permanence to the more exciting world outside. He might as well have added that membership of the golf club would keep he and his brother from Class A drugs and possibly prevent them from becoming mercenaries in some far-off conflict, for all the subtlety of the remark.

'And six,' he added, adopting the air of a man who felt he had an easy command of the situation, 'you can go back to that idiot who wouldn't let you on his course in Cornwall and demand to play.'

'You have a point,' I said. And he did have a point. The brochure showed an alluring scene of 4 satisfied golfers returning from what had evidently been an intensely fulfilling round, the evening sun slanting in on them as they made their way towards the clubhouse for cock-tails. The inference was that this was all about fitness, about well-being, about honest competition and ageless camaraderie. It would be some time before we realised that the norm was rather different, that the sun would have to be very bright indeed to shine into the kind of undergrowth that we were going to be frequenting over the next few months, and that camaraderie tends to be in short supply when a middle aged bloke is making a complete arse of himself. As for the cocktails, that notion was for the birds.

The adjudication process was one that would be familiar to most families. No one apart from the Undergraduate had really come up with anything else attractive enough to be taken seriously. My younger son, the Student, had made an impassioned pitch as to how a second hand car should be considered 'an experience', rather than a 'possession', if it was looked at philosophically, but no one bought it, either the argument or the car. My wife, the Artist, had weighed up the personal advantage of a fortnight on an Indian Ocean beach against the long term benefit of keeping her children off the streets and decided in favour of the latter. She realised that what she might lose in the occasional absence of the men in her life, she would gain by the comfort of knowing that they were not up to anything worse.

'So that's a "yes", is it?' asked the Undergraduate.

'But the cost?! I bet you never even asked him for a deal. I bet he's gagging for new members, and that he'll ...'

'He's waiving 50% of the joining fee, and giving us 19 months for the price of 12. Still reckon I can't negotiate?'

There was a pause, during which I started the painful process of surrendering an existing prejudice.

'If you give me your bank card, I'll go and sort it for you this afternoon,' he said.

And in those 16 words were summarised at least 3 of the hidden secrets of my 20 year stab at parenthood. The graceful acceptance of defeat when it becomes inevitable; the knowledge that your bank details and pin number are a well-known family secret; and the fact that it always seems to turn out that parental money is, in fact, only ever spent as a direct favour to the parent.

The die was cast and the Rubicon crossed. The Seychelles trip, the fortnight in the Alps, the rock festival and the crates of fine wines were all consigned to history and the recycling bin. From that day we had a family membership of the Southdowns Golf Club.

Up until this point in my life, golf had fallen into the category of things like coarse fishing and supporting Manchester United, in that I was aware that millions of people ended up doing them, but none of them, when pressed, could ever quite say why. I felt that it was a game played by the kind of people who simply did things better than I did, and who might also just be crying out for a source of authority and hierarchy to give gravitas to their unstructured lives. And because in my various forays into the game over the last thirty years or so, I had never played it regularly enough to make that step change to some any sort of consistency.

Having said all that, there is an undeniable beauty about an empty golf course, and an undefinable sense of personal challenge lying deep within it. Its effect on me had always been to pull back the curtain fractionally, temptingly even, on a world that existed beyond the pavement and the streetlight, and, like all of life, the most exciting bits were the parts you couldn't see from the road.

In a world of twenty-four hour news, uninvited noise and joyless over-crowding, the golf course seemed to stick two well manicured fingers up at the crowding deadlines and whisper to me: 'Come over here and live a bit'.

*

Even by his standards, the Cabinet Maker looked a complete mess.

He was sitting on the high, chalky bank of a tiny lane at the foot of the South Downs, waving his foot in the air in tiny, pathetic circles.

'It's gone,' he said with finality.

'What? Really gone? Or gone in an 'I'm-a-bit-puffed-and-could-do-with-a-few-minutes-injury-time' sort of way?'

'Really gone,' he said. 'I'm going to need a lift home'.

He had the air of a broken man who had gone into the newsagents at 5 in the afternoon and discovered that the only paper left was the *Daily Express*.

'I can't believe that we signed up for this thing,' he said for the fiftieth time

'*We* didn't sign up for it. You signed us all up for it. Back in December when you were all miserable and needed a challenge. And anyway, it's only 13 miles, and we're already up to 7.' I looked at his pallid ankle and accompanying foot, rotating around against the grass. 'Well, 5 in your case. But it's 4 more than you could do a month ago.'

Together with the Banker, and in a spirit of careless discovery, we had entered into the 2016 Bath Half Marathon for the second year running. Having sworn blind that none of us would practise alone, weekday evenings were in fact spent with each of us slyly, and individually, running along suitably darkened lanes, in preparation for our runs together at the weekends. At which point we would strenuously deny that we had done any such thing, whilst wondering why the other two were making such light weather of the challenging run we had set ourselves. To be fair, we had a number of distance runs under our belt at this point, and to be fairer still, the Cabinet Maker had led the way on each of them. He had an irritatingly effective lope, albeit one like an elderly but determined hyena with its eye on lunch on some distant savannah.

I drove him home and then sat at his kitchen table nursing a blue and white Pompey FC mug full of tea. The brush with such excellence as that mug implied was almost suffocating. Portsmouth was the kind of club that you supported only if you absolutely couldn't help it and the Cabinet Maker really couldn't help it. Its glory days could be compressed into a handful of months nearly 70 years ago, when it won a couple of things. Since then it had been on a steepening decline, punctuating the descent with occasional bankruptcies and the nightmare of being managed by Harry Rednapp.

'It's bollocks, mate. I can't do it.' He only ever used the word 'mate' if he wanted to emphasise his working class credentials or make a serious point. I gave him credit for this being the latter. 'I don't want to spend the entire summer hobbling around, so I'm going to call it a day. Sorry. Someone else can have my entry.'

And so it was that the Cabinet Maker's short relationship with distance running buried itself in the metaphorical sand. For a moment I almost felt sorry for him, but it quickly passed. He had enjoyed an equally brief but rather more successful relationship with stand-up comedy back in the day and he had got over that OK. 'But just don't tell the Banker just yet. He's running tomorrow, and there's every chance he'll do himself in and have to bail before I do. He looked like a broken man on Iping Common last Saturday. I don't want to be the first one to bin it.'

The fact is that we were all a bit bored with the running thing. First time out at the Great South Run it had been an adventure, as had the initial Bath Half Marathon. There was a certain nobility in fighting back the years, something really quite optimistic in keeping to a vague training schedule that delivered your body on race day in a far better condition than it was accustomed to. It was like middle-aged cycling, but without all the luminous lycra and the endless technical running commentary and investment in state of the art machinery to gain a fraction of a second that cyclists are prone to. In the act of running past people under half ones age came a strange pride, even if the pride was inevitably followed by an even stranger fall. Besides, it was as British as killing off the entire population of a small rural village in the name of a TV detective show.

A thought occurred to me.

'Tell me everything you know about golf'.

'Cynthia,' the Cabinet Maker replied after a short pause. 'They're all called Cynthia. Or Graham if they're blokes. And they're builders. And hairdressers. And they like rules. And blazers. And they do stuff for cash.' He considered the matter more empirically for an instant and added 'Tossers, mainly!' before enquiring why I'd asked the question.

'Nothing,' I said. 'Just curious, that's all'.

*

Two miles across town, and at the same time, the Undergraduate had presented himself at the Banker's house for some career advice.

As a rule, undergraduates enjoy career advice rather more than they enjoy the prospect of an actual career. For a start, advice allows them to dream, without any of the inconvenience of it being for real, or ending up with a rejection letter. Then there is the faint but alluring possibility that whoever is doing the advising knows someone who knows someone who works somewhere next door to somewhere else that offers internships, or even jobs. At the same time successful people, like the Banker, enjoy dispensing advice, for doing so to youngsters allows them to feel wise beyond their years, and not a bull-shitter at all. And, as every parent knows, advising someone else's child, like running someone else's company, is a whole heap more fun than trying to do it to your own.

The older man had taken the younger one under his professional wing over the last few years, recognising in him his own slightly chaotic arrival into adult life, and wanted to help him navigate through that ghastly transition where student life first meets full time work, and runs screaming for the hills.

The Banker looked at the kitchen clock, and then at the fridge.

'Bit early for a beer? What do you reckon?'

'Well, I'm not really drinking at the moment, but I'll have one if you are'. This was important, as the Banker subscribed to the point of view that held that periods of abstinence should be reserved only for the kind of people who washed their cars at weekends.

Mythology now insists that the pair of them then spoke a great deal about the banking system, about asset finance, bonds and gilts and the velocity of money supply. And that they left no stone unturned on the subject of debt, both corporate and national, hedge funds, insurance premiums and credit ratings. And that it must have been all of 15 minutes before the Undergraduate said out of the blue:

'You really ought to come and have a round at Southdowns. We've just joined.'

The Banker's thoughts were elsewhere at the time, quite possibly with the bonus structure currently operating at his place of employment. Recognising that the last quarter of an hour had exhausted the younger man's attention span he welcomed the weekend back into his life.

'I hadn't marked you down as a golfer,' he said.

'Nor had I. But we've decided to give it a go, as a family. Do you fancy a crack at it? I'm sure you could come as my guest.'

The Banker carefully weighed the options. An outright rejection, as he should have given to the distance running scheme two years before, would protect him from something that financial people fear more than almost anything – making a tit of himself – but would deprive him of potential fun with his mates. An outright acceptance, whilst doubtless a fine career move within the bank, would put him on the route to endless time wasting, expensive equipment and thrashing around in deep sand traps.

'Sounds good to me,' he said. 'When do we start?'

*

The first thing to learn about golf, if you are a pheasant, is not to spend too much of your life hanging around on driving ranges[1], irrespective of whether you're in season or not. In the event, the old resident cock bird became the first minor casualty of our new quartet when we went up to 'hit a few balls' the following weekend.

It was a breathlessly sunny day, the type that is normally reserved for the Tuesday following a wet Bank Holiday weekend, and the four of us had come together to get some practise in before unleashing the full potential ghastliness of our game on to the Southdowns course proper.

The original idea had been that we would tackle this adventure as a family unit, but we were already discovering that the different component parts of that unit had equally differing ideas as to what constituted a good use of a Sunday afternoon. For now, it was the Cabinet Maker, the Banker, the Undergraduate and me.

Much could be told about the individuals in our group by the manner of their arrival at the range.

The Banker arrived in a capacious piece of German metal-ware with two large exhaust pipes, and many bits of lettering on the back. On the rear screen sat discreet stickers notifying the world of his membership of a

---

[1]For the benefit of non golfers, a driving range is a practise ground where your strokes don't count and where, consequently, most of us play our best shots.

couple of prestigious organisations, and on the calf-skin passenger seat lay a very slightly creased copy of the *Financial Times*. He was casually immaculate, in an understated black polo shirt and matching trousers, and he had the unhurried aura of a man who both expected and intended to be rather good at the new things he tried. When he waved his foot under the car boot, which then duly opened for him, and even more duly impressed his friends, we were fully expecting to see a full set of state of the art clubs. We didn't. What we actually saw was his grandfather's old 3 wood, a venerable hickory club that had probably last seen action some 30 plus years ago.

'Can I borrow some clubs, please?' he said.

The Cabinet Maker arrived in a van with two small dogs in a cage in the back and dragged out an ancient tarpaulin bag of clubs, also from another era. Where the Banker had a copy of the *FT* on his seat, the Cabinet Maker had a B & Q catalogue on his, and where the former looked like he had just come off a fashion shoot, the latter looked like he had just been laying a small brick retaining wall in his vegetable garden, which he had. He dusted some cement powder off his trousers and eyed up the Banker.

'You've been practising, haven't you?'

The Undergraduate turned up with me in my car, accompanied by a vague, hungover smile. He was clasping a phone in his right hand, and wearing a beany hat, and a tee shirt that said disobliging things about some political party or other. The strains of Edward Sharpe and the Magnetic Zeros filtered out of his head phones and up into the quiet Sussex afternoon like bonfire smoke. He had found some huge and ancient driver in amongst a load of junk at home and was already brandishing it like a Samurai sword. If the Banker's motivation for the next half hour or so was the pursuit of excellence, then the Undergraduate's was to inflict the maximum amount of damage to the largest possible number of balls.

We all inserted our tokens into the dispensing machine and duly received our bucket of 60 or so golf balls. These were not the gleaming white ones that we might have had in mind, but tatty and soft ones that looked as though they had overwintered in a cold and wet landfill site in Kazakhstan. Although there was plenty of room on the range for all of us to drive away simultaneously, we agreed that it would be much more fun to subject each individual to the scrutiny, and to the possibly helpful comments, of his colleagues. I went first.

In competitive situations, body language and aggressive intent weigh almost as heavily as technical competence, so I decided on the no-nonsense, no rehearsal approach; I would simply set my ball on a tee, forgo any warm up or practise swings and let the others marvel at the distance and straightness of my very first hit.

'When I'm in a zone, I don't think about the shot or the wind or the distance or the gallery or anything,' Mark Calcavecchia once said. 'I just pull a club and swing'. So I just pulled a club, and I swung.

Apart from one tiny detail, the shot did exactly what I had intended. I would argue that it looked good and felt good and that, by rights, a few seconds later it should be coming to rest against a marker board with the numbers '200' applied to it. The one tiny detail, that of my having missed the ball completely, was probably caused, on reflection, by my having been looking directly up at the 200 yard marker board at exactly the time when I should have been looking down at the ball. It has to be said that this small detail had defined such golf as I had played up until now, and would go on doing so for many months to come. Silence is often the cruellest reaction, and silence is what I got.

The Cabinet Maker, it turned out, followed the Payne Stewart dictum ('A bad attitude is worse than a bad swing'), and announced before he played his first shot not only how far it was going to go, but against which little sapling out on the range his ball would finish. He stared out at the wide blue yonder, swished his club a couple of times in a manner that denoted total control, and then stepped up to address his ball. He could have saved himself time; his ball finished exactly where it had started, and exactly where my own ball had finished.

'Practise swing,' he said, as if that explained everything, and then deposited a feeble scuff into the long grass a few feet in front. It seemed almost impossible that someone with all the normal limbs, and in possession of enough co-ordination to, say, allow him legally to drive a car, could not hit an elevated and stationary ball further than he could throw a filled suitcase.

Equally, having seen the Banker's first three shots, it seemed almost impossible to believe that he had not gained some underhand experience. His was a languid and measured swing which, in its modest way, worked every time. 75 yards. 100 yards. 125 yards. Even on the driving range, with a large bucket of balls available and with no cost to a bad stroke, he did 4 or 5 practise swings for each shot, and a rather smug holding of the pose afterwards, like a Test cricketer who has just unfurled a sumptuous cover drive.

'Wanker,' said the Cabinet Maker, and it was hard for a reasonable man not to agree with the sentiment.

That just left the Undergraduate, who had to be awakened from a reverie of snap-chatting a picture of his father with an applied beard and Hitler moustache to their mutual friends. It has to be said that what followed was as close to awesome as a man can get while still being dominantly incompetent.

On its massive backswing, the head of his driver had gone so far round that it was pointing downwards to the ground below his left hip before it began its journey back again. Now separated geographically from the ball it was supposed to hit by a large body, it started its journey back behind his neck, making a whistling noise as it did so. All the laws of dynamics suggested that this would end in injury, or at the very least, humiliation. Instead of which, it seemed to make two or three minor alterations in its direction before it swung through a perfect arc and hit his ball smack in the middle, with all the savage power a vigorous young man can impart before he starts to worry about old shoulder injuries, unpaid mortgages and failure.

The ball left its tee like a rocket, seeming to go some distance before it actually started climbing. It was still in the ascent mode when it passed the Banker's longest drive 60 foot below it, and still had about 50 yards of roll left in it when it finally came to earth. Brutal. Straight. 275 yards. The Undergraduate tried not to look surprised, whilst the remaining three of us tried to make it look like we hadn't been watching.

'Tosser,' said the Cabinet Maker.

And if he had stopped there, stopped playing golf

altogether, the Undergraduate would have had a great career. If he had artlessly climbed back into the car and said 'Thank you, gentlemen, but this is not for me', he could have looked back at a sport where he had only competed at the highest level. But he didn't. Like the rest of us, he piled through the bucket of balls spraying them in an arc that included the 2nd fairway, 90 degrees to the left, and a clump of oaks 90 degrees to the right. Because that is what sport does to you. In amongst all the misery, the failure, the expense and the underachievement, arises just enough beauty, just enough magnificence, just enough perfection, to cloud your mind into thinking it could always be like that, and into ploughing on.

The Undergraduate had arrived at his last ball, and smacked it on its top edge with awesome power, imparting an extreme topspin to it. Freed of the need to go high, it hit the ground in front and accelerated off in a generally westerly direction hugging the ground and running smack into a passing cock pheasant. Although the bird was knocked off its feet, it quickly picked itself up and limped off into the nearby shelter belt.

'I think we've seen enough,' announced the Banker when the Undergraduate suggested we bought another few buckets of balls, not for the last time protecting his own early psychological advantage. 'I'll buy you all a beer'.

*

I hadn't yet introduced myself to the Clubhouse bar, and didn't think that this was either the day, the group, or the circumstances in which to first do so. We had survived 50 minutes on the driving range, and to spend more time here might just be tempting fate. We headed north to the Duke of Cumberland instead, an idyllic watering hole high up on the hill behind the course.

What followed was one of those pivotal half hours in life during which you begin to discover whether the thing that you have just done was merely that, a thing that you have just done, or whether it was the start of something more significant. There was no doubt that our distance running days had petered out in a rash of Deep Heat and broken promises, and equally little doubt that we needed something to replace it. After all, life was too short not to be forever learning to be not very good at something or other new.

Up until this point, the four of us had harboured enough inherited prejudices about golf and the people who played it for us to try our hands at almost anything else. The way we collectively looked at it was that golf was a potentially excellent game spoiled by the extreme versions of its own etiquette, rules and, occasionally, its players. In our minds eye, where others might have been able to see a magnificent links course early on a fresh summer morning, all we could imagine were grim-faced pairs looming out of the mist and demanding to play through if we were a bit slow. And, where kinder people than us could imagine the satisfaction of honest competition, all we could conjure up in our minds were accusations of chicanery in the Monthly Medal. Besides, of all the sports and pastimes available out there, golf seemed to be the one most wedded to money and most entrapped within its own unchanging traditions. Having said all that, it was also without question a sport that allowed true friendships the time and space to develop within it, and this was its ultimate appeal.

We were ultimately brought into line by the fact that we each knew and liked many individual golfers, which must mean that there had to be a hinterland of normality out there even if we had not yet spotted it. 'People,' as George Eliot helpfully pointed out, 'are almost always better than their neighbours think they are', a sentiment that suggested we were being both hasty and unfair in our early judgements on the matter. We should allow the next twelve months to slow-cook that opinion for us, rather than flash-frying it over a pint of San Miguel in the Duke of Cumberland.

In the days and weeks that followed our family decision to join the club, the Artist had dabbled on the driving range a couple of times before announcing that she probably had more compelling things to do with her time. She was not competitive enough to take it at all seriously, and not so disturbed by the ageing process as to require her to keep having to find ways of reversing it. A little bit of her also recognised that if this was my mid-life crisis, there were many worse ways it could manifest itself. At the same time the Student, who was up to his eyes in A Levels and political theories, told us that the game was too long, too structured and too competitive for him, and said that he would join for the occasional round so long as we didn't make him a member, or buy him a stupid golfing sweater.

'Anyway,' he announced as he helped himself to a large glass of Beaujolais, 'I think I may be becoming a Marxist.' It explained everything.

So we downgraded the family membership to individual ones for the Undergraduate and me. The Banker, true to type, joined up at the achingly prestigious Goodwood course a few miles south on the Downs; and the Cabinet Maker, also true to type, joined up at a nine hole pitch and putt adjacent to a local school, where he could play all the golf he wanted, tips and lessons included, for £160 a year.

Our resulting quartet was an unlikely one, but it was solid. It was based on the three older members forgetting to complete the process of growing up, and on the younger one failing to resent the fact that they hadn't. At an age where most people tend to run screaming for the hills rather than spend time with people in middle age, the Undergraduate seemed to find our pathetic attempts to recreate childhood diverting, attractive even. He was also smart enough to know that we didn't operate under quite such onerous financial constraints as he did, and that his inner man should benefit accordingly. Besides, we all needed a challenge.

Over the last few years, this co-operation had dipped into cricket, canoeing, tennis, raft racing, clay pigeon shooting, bee-keeping and many other activities besides, all of which had been defined by an extraordinary absence of anything approaching excellence. True enough, the Cabinet Maker had built an exquisite canoe, as one might expect him to, but when out on the Rivers Arun, Rother and Thames, the four of us had routinely done all we could to sink it, along with any craft that happened to be in its vague proximity. On one occasion, we had even had the foresight to alert the RNLI that we were approaching the sea on the ebb Spring tide at Littlehampton, and, whilst not in immediate trouble yet, were not completely sure that we would be able to stop as we came out of the bottleneck where the Arun meets the English Channel. And, true enough, I had gone so far as to co-establish and run a cricket team that had lasted nearly a third of a century, but it remained a team that had oppositions licking their lips in expectation when they realised that we were next up on the fixture list.[2]

---

[2]Different adventures, described in a different book: *Not Out First Ball*

Of the fact that the quartet was fuelled by beer and wine, there can be no serious doubt, but it was also enabled to do the things it did through the resigned patience, and occasional participation, of its wider family members.

'We need to aim for something,' said the Undergraduate, who was personally aiming at being bought a second pint. 'We will only get somewhere if we work out what we want from it. How about we each come up with a target for the group, and then come back here in a year's time and see what happened.' Sometimes, we found ourselves taking what the Undergraduate was saying seriously, simply because, through the lack of direct comparisons being drawn, his age made him less of a competitive threat than the others.

We thought about what he had said. Over three decades ago, when Isis was still a tributary of the Thames in Oxford, and Donald Trump just a builder with a silly name, I had run a marathon in 2 hours 58 minutes, having discovered a sport at which no technical skill was required, just a breathless ability to put one foot in front of another about 20,000 times. Later on, I had aimed to complete a full marathon in less than 4 hours, a half marathon in less than 105 minutes, and I had remained pitifully distant from either objective. We had all promised to navigate the Thames from source to sea, to win the annual River Rother Raft Race and to achieve an annual bowling average that was lower than our batting average. We had never got close to any of these objectives. However, in our hearts we knew the Undergraduate was right: if we were going to get anywhere in this most technical of games, if we were going to avoid wasting a year of time and money, we had to immerse ourselves in it to some extent, and have the humility to learn it properly.

The Banker, who had learned his humility in the City of London, gazed up for a while at a stuffed fish on the wall and pondered. 'We should all end the year with a handicap[3]. That's mine.' I thought about the grim-faced secretary on that Cornish Golf Course, and gave it my whole-hearted support.

'At least one of us should break 100 for 18 holes by mid-summer's day'. That was my own contribution. There again, that had been my contribution for each of the thirty-five years I had been an occasional golfer.

[3]Golfers need handicap certificates in order to be allowed to play on nice courses where they are not members; they are, in effect, golfing passports whose authority applies all over the world. A handicap theoretically demonstrates a measurable level of competence that can then, among other things, dictate how many strokes you might receive, or give, in a match. The lower the number, the better the player. Handicaps for men start at 28, meaning that they would be expected to get round a course in the normal 72 shots plus a further 28, meaning 100. Ladies' handicaps begin at 36, which would mean that she is expected to go round in 72 plus 36, which is 108. A 'scratch' golfer, male or female, is expected to go round a course in 72, but I have never met one of these.

'How about at least one of us winning at least one proper match in a proper competition within the year?' offered the Cabinet Maker.

The Undergraduate was somewhere deep in the bowels of his phone, trying to find out just how badly Fulham had been beaten that afternoon, so we left it at the three objectives.

'Tom,' said the Banker, not for the last time in the year. 'Put that fucking phone away!'

Chapter 2

A GOOD WALK SPOILED

'Without obsession, life is nothing.'
John Waters

The Big Easy has the most beautiful swing of them all.

Maybe less so now than in his heyday in the early 1990s, but, for me, to watch it was once to dream of playing golf, and of playing it well. This was a game about which I knew very little, and cared rather less, but something about the way Ernie Els conducted himself on a course, his economy of effort, his exquisite timing and his phlegmatic approach, shone a spotlight into a better sporting place. Others may have, and indeed did, achieve more, but it was watching Els lighting up the championship courses he played on that made me know that I would one day want to play the game, too. He was one superlative short of having it all, and I loved him all the more for that final missing bit. Faldo was more remorselessly, dourly, single minded; Ballasteros was more explosively brilliant and Tiger Woods was all arrogant perfection, but it was Els who initially recruited me to the game, and who changed my mind. On the 3rd day at the 2002 British Open, when conditions were so bad that half the field carded rounds in the mid eighties, Els set himself up for the Claret Jug with a near flawless 72. I was only watching the round on TV by accident and because the cricket had been rained off but, little by little, I became mesmerised by his genial demeanour, and that beautiful swing.

Then there was the whole internal battle thing. For someone like me, all of whose sports involved moving balls, I simply couldn't understand how a still ball sport could deliver the excitement it did, nor how a man as mentally strong as Greg Norman could implode at the 1996 Masters when all he had to do was hit a stationary ball in a straight line a few times. I, who had thrown tennis racquets over the netting and squash racquets against the wall in my time and gone so far as to hurl my cricket bat into a tributary of the River Loire, couldn't work out how an activity so placid as golf could have Sergio Garcia hurling his left shoe into the gallery in fury, or Henrik Stenson chucking his putter into the adjoining lake. Viewed from a distance, golf seemed to lack any emotional potential whatsoever, and I just couldn't understand why people got so excited by it. Underneath the surface, though, there seethed a maelstrom of basic human challenges.

I might not have known it then, but I do now. At Grid Reference 901228 (Map sheet 197), there is a hybrid club stuck fast, 60 foot up an oak tree, which stands testament to my subsequent education on the subject. The last I saw of it before it was hidden by summer foliage, it was providing the central structural architecture of a rook's nest.

Any investigation as to why this game matters so much to the people who play it needs to start with where it came from.

*

At some point in history, someone thought it might be a diverting idea to build a game out of the concept of getting a ball of compacted feathers into a small, distant hole by hitting it there using long bits of tree. Doing things like that is, fundamentally, why we became top animal. After all, an iguana would never think of that.

As a statement of just how far Man had come since his days of survival-based hunter gathering, it is really quite impressive that he even got round to considering the matter, let alone finding the time and energy to do something about it. But then Man has been equally inventive at finding myriad other diverting things to do with spherical things, so much so that he has become as much defined by sport as he has by science, by cooking or by parking his money with a Panamanian law firm. Doing things with balls, be they big, small or any size in between, has become his evolutionary way of releasing the competitive urges that would otherwise have him thinking up ingenious ways to kill the warrior caste of any opposing tribe, and then to run off with their women. It is a form of liberal progress admired by all but a few.

For, other than in the *Comment* pages of the Guardian and among certain teaching unions, the human race generally accepts that healthy competition goes hand in hand with staying at the top of the food chain. Throughout history, the spoils have gone to the fastest, the strongest and the most cunning, whilst the other 98% of us have had to come up with coping strategies to deal with our failure. Human ingenuity eventually saw to it that we turned this inferiority into some kind of advantage by deriving our pleasure from watching these demi-gods perform for our entertainment, rather than skulking miserably at home pretending they didn't exist. Thus did our forebears sit at the Sanctuary of Zeus at Olympia, four centuries before Christ, and watch the heroic efforts of the muscle-bound wrestlers, boxers and discus throwers in the *pankration* unfold, just as we now routinely follow huge people in red nylon shirts at The Lakeside Country Club, throwing a sequence of three very small javelins into a particular spot in a 17 and three quarter inch round sisal board [nearly] eight long feet away from them, all while quaffing copious pints of beer. The excellence of it all is close to breath-taking.

So sport emerged as a cunning way of diverting the warrior caste from killing each other in the fratricidal conflicts that ravaged the world from the cradle of civilisation onwards. The logic ran that, just because you hated your neighbouring tribe, it wasn't always necessary to kill and maim them, although Millwall supporters have made their own valiant attempt to circumvent this concept of progress over the years. Fighting proficiency slowly morphed into less lethal formats of combat, where the opposition didn't actually have to die in order to have made a success of the day.

A happy progression runs from the *retiarii* in the Roman Coliseum, through the jousting knights of the late Middle Ages, to the competitors in the Masters at Augusta, with an agreeable reduction in fatalities as its determining feature. It turned out that we could express our fierce tribal loyalties from the pitch, rather than from the battlefield, and drown our disappointment in the pub, rather than under our widow's tears. It all explains how properly excited the nation became in the 30th Olympiad back in 2012, and the point should not be lost that sport has possibly been just as effective as the discovery of penicillin in the matter of keeping people alive.

It also gives men something to talk about on Mondays.

Records of a game that looks pretty much like golf date back to around 1000BC, and its origins are variously and vigorously claimed by the Chinese, the Egyptians, the Romans, the Dutch and the Scots. Idle research suggests that it was really the Dutch who came up with what passes for modern golf, but it was the canny Scots who successfully constructed a mythology that convinced just enough influential Americans to allow it to become received wisdom in the bit of the world that counted. Once it became received wisdom that Scotland had given the world golf, it became very hard to argue that they hadn't and, on the basis of that piece of creativity, the game became theirs until the Americans wanted it for themselves. Suffice it to say that, round about 1457, someone was recorded as hacking a ball round a Scottish field, probably closely followed by someone called Trump trying to buy the place up to build an international golf and convention centre. It didn't matter anyway as James II of Scotland had the game outlawed for a long while as it distracted young men from training with sharp weapons to keep the English out of their country, something Nicola Sturgeon now does with enviable commitment and rather less violence.

Nothing much happened after that until 1744, when the first known rules of golf were set down by the Gentlemen Golfers of Edinburgh. There were 13 of these rules, and they still form the basis of the regulations followed by most golfers, but routinely ignored by the Banker. The gist of them is that you use a number of different sticks to propel a little ball from a start point in one place to a small hole in a lawn in another. In as few shots as you can manage. And then do it eighteen times. To achieve this you are allowed a bag of no more than fourteen sticks, of which at least eight are utterly pointless but seem to add gravitas to your game. Your bag may also contain as many balls as you care to carry, plus tees, a glove and a pork pie or two. You may make your ball easier to hit by raising it up on a tiny platform at the start, by cleaning it, or by claiming something called 'winter rules' that allows you to put it in an altogether better place at will. Or not, depending on who you are playing with.

Back then, it was as simple as this:

'1.   *You must Tee your Ball within a Club's length of the Hole.*

2.   *Your Tee must be upon the Ground.*

3.   *You are not to change the Ball which you Strike off the Tee.*

4.   *You are not to remove Stones, Bones or any Break Club, for the sake of playing your Ball, Except upon the fair Green and that only / within a Club's length of your Ball.*

5.   *If your Ball comes among watter, or any wattery filth, you are at liberty to take out your Ball & bringing it behind the hazard and Teeing it, you may play it with any Club and allow your Adversary a Stroke for so getting out your Ball.*

6.   *If your Balls be found any where touching one another, You are to lift the first Ball, till you play the last.*

7. *At Holling, you are to play your Ball honestly for the Hole, and not to play upon your Adversary's Ball, not lying in your way to the Hole.*

8. *If you should lose your Ball, by it's being taken up, or any other way, you are to go back to the Spot, where you struck last, & drop another Ball, And allow your adversary a Stroke for the misfortune.*

9. *No man at Holling his Ball, is to be allowed, to mark his way to the Hole with his Club, or anything else.*

10. *If a Ball be stopp'd by any Person, Horse, Dog or anything else, The Ball so stop'd must be play'd where it lyes.*

11. *If you draw your Club in Order to Strike, & proceed so far in the Stroke as to be e Accounted a Stroke.*

12. *He whose Ball lyes farthest from the Hole is obliged to play first.*

13. *Neither Trench, Ditch or Dyke, made for the preservation of the Links, nor the Scholar's Holes, or the Soldier's Lines, Shall be accounted a Hazard; But the Ball is to be taken out teed /and play'd with any Iron Club.'*

Instinctively, I liked the idea of 'wattery filth', which was just as well, given how much of the next year I was going to spend trying to retrieve my ball from it.

There are then all sorts of penalties for things you do wrong on the way, but these need not detain us for now. Most golf courses are about 4 miles long, and have 18 holes dotted around, each one of which allows you a humorously small number of strokes in which to sink your ball. Due to the Law of Unintended Consequences prevailing as it always seems to, good golfers tend to be unhealthier and financially poorer than bad golfers, as they take 50% less exercise on each round, and get 50% less value per shot whilst doing so.

In 1825, Mr Pringle convinced an initially sceptical public that looking faintly ridiculous should not be the preserve of awkward men on stag parties, and developed a range of colourful patterned sweaters for golfers. A surprising number of them thought that he was actually being serious, and so started a trend unique among world sports that still exists to this day. We may get round to examining clothing and equipment in a little more detail later in the book, but on the off-chance that the Ritalin wears off before you get to that point and you feel the need to get out there and start the big shop-up right now, the basic rule is to look as stupid as you dare, whilst still being able to walk and swing a club and climb out of a bunker. The Cabinet Maker will show you how.

Later in the same century, the English adopted golf with a passion. The number of courses rising from 12 in 1880 to over 1000 at the dawn of World War 1. The idea caught on rapidly around the British Empire and also in any European holiday resort where British tourists went in considerable numbers. Like most British sports it eventually trickled downwards from the highest social strata with acres of leisure time on their bored hands. It was subsequently exported and, as usual with our finest exports, we then found a bewildering variety of methods of being defeated at it by foreigners. At the time of writing, nearly 2% of the UK's land area is taken up with golf courses of one sort or another, and there are 2989 of them. Make that a few less, actually, as the high water mark is long past and they are now closing at a surprising rate.

Golf arrived in the USA towards the end of the 18th century, and a handful of clubs argue to this day over the honour of having been the first. They now have over 10000 courses to console themselves with, and lose themselves in, when the sheer responsibility of being the world's top nation gets too much for them. The Americans now effectively own the game of golf, as they do most of modern culture. They have added touches to the original game, such as the cries of 'Yee-haa', 'Way to go' or 'Attaboy' when a fellow golfer does something clever. (The Cabinet Maker once shouted 'way to go!' during a round at Southdowns, but it turned out it was the final part of an instruction he was giving to his ball.)

To be fair, they also balanced the sulking brilliance of Tiger

Woods with the sheer genius of players like Jack Nicklaus, and the occasionally mindless Ryder Cup crowds with the treat of Payne Stewart's sensational trousers.

Nowadays, golf is a truly international phenomenon. There are over 32000 courses worldwide to select from and there are only 2 countries in the world where you couldn't get a game if you wanted to – the Maldives and Vatican City. Small wonder then that the four of us were so keen to get stuck into it all.

There is even a British Golf Museum located at the Royal and Ancient at St Andrews, but I suspect that deep down we all know exactly the kind of people that we would meet there, and we had best pass it by. At least at this stage, while we are still unclear whether we will like golf, or golf will like us.

*

There is only one vital piece of equipment in the hacker's stuttering journey into the game of golf, and it is not what you think it is.

It is not the latest Taylor Made M1 Driver at £499, nor is it the 12 pack of Callaway supersoft golf balls. It is not, sadly, the Royal and Awesome 'King of Diamond' trouser, nice though that would be to have, nor yet the Laser Bushnell Rangefinder. It is none of the thousand and one accessories that you can lay your hands on in every Pro's shop or golf emporium up and down the country. It is not even the Calvin Klein 2016 golf hat.

No, the only important piece of equipment to bring with you to a golf course is the person, or people, you intend to play with. Get that right and the way opens to unsullied delight. Get it wrong, and every story they ever tell you about the awfulness of this most loved and hated of sports will come frighteningly and unarguably true. The stereotypically grim golfer will be with us always. They will be there in male and female form, laying down the law, arguing on little points of order and etiquette, positioning themselves for social promotion, and tea-potting their constant disapproval from adjacent fairways. But they are merely incidental, like summer rain showers, and it is entirely your fault if they intrude on your enjoyment. The biggest discovery of our new adventure was a tedious unscrambling of the old prejudice about the people who played this game: 90% of them are lovely, just like the rest of the human race. They leave home on a Saturday morning with the same ambitions, tolerate the same triumphs and disasters, and run into the brick wall of mediocrity just like we do, albeit at a rather higher level.

The ideal playing partner, or opponent, looks, chronologically speaking, like this:

1. They leave home with a slight feeling of guilt, possibly hungover, and permanently equipped with a salary cheque that is too small, and a mortgage that is too big. They do not oil up in a well-manicured Jaguar, slide out and look you up and down before saying rather too smoothly 'How's it going, buddy?'.

2. They fumble around in a boot that is full of detritus from the last three family holidays and a punctured cycle wheel that has been there for more than a year, and they pull out a bag that is an amalgam of '50% off' purchases from 9 different shops. They do not wave their foot suggestively under the boot of their car until it springs expensively open revealing a full set of 6 month old Cobra Golf King Forged clubs, each one gleaming in the morning sun, and the whole lot in a leather bag that has rather too many labels saying 'Wentworth'.

3. Their dress is borderline acceptable, chinos rather than jeans, coupled with a none too clean pink Gant polo shirt that they found in a child's sports bag whilst he was away at University. They hope it will not rain, as they only have another child's Duke Of Edinburgh expedition waterproof, which is 3 sizes too small. They do not pitch up festooned with the latest branded gilet, teamed up with £200 Ping trousers and a $50 golf hat they bought in a Texan pro's shop.

4. They don't mind where you park. If the car park is full and the Lady Captain is in Huddersfield having her hair done, they would consider it logical to park right there, and not see it as a prelude to a diplomatic crisis. Parking hierarchy is to golf, I discovered many times along the way, what insignia are to military officers: a marked space near the clubhouse announces to the world your ascent within the golfing tribe, a sort of mark on the greasy pole of social progress that most of us never need to aspire to.

5. They understand that there is an extensive tidal margin in this sport where worthy tradition meets pointless regulation and that, as a new player, you will constantly find yourself trying to establish in your own mind into which side of the metaphorical seaweed you have pitched up. They help explain it.

6. They hunger for a bacon bap. All nice people secretly hunger for a bacon bap, even when religion and medical advice forbids it. There are few conflicts in the modern world that could not be ushered towards peace more effectively by the artful deployment of bacon baps. Think about it, Vladimir Putin.

7. They ache for matchplay, rather than strokeplay,(*)[4]

---

[4]For non-golfers, strokeplay is a version of the game in which every stroke counts, whilst in matchplay you only count each hole won or lost. The worst you can lose in matchplay is 10 down, and 8 to play. The worst you can lose in strokeplay is too painful to contemplate.

for then the third consecutive hook off into the corn-field alongside the second fairway only signifies one lost hole, not a lost round. They do not know what Stapleford is, but wish they did, as it sounds kind of comforting.[5]

8. They will walk and carry their own clubs if they are young enough and healthy enough to do so. If they do have reason to take a buggy they will challenge it with the most extreme gradients and situations they can conjure up.

9. They hold the pose if they do a passable practise shot, for they know deep down that this may be the only decent shot they play on the hole, and they do not want it to pass unappreciated.

10. If your own ball is lying in an impossible position, deep within the root system of a 1000 year old oak, for example, and you are almost in tears, they don't just stand there suggesting club selections. They accidentally kick it back on to the fairway and then apologise for doing so. Their own happiness is closely linked to your happiness.

11. They turn their phone off. Right off. Unless, of course, there are important scores to catch up with on Cricinfo, or an adored maiden aunt is on her last legs.

[5]Stapleford is a scoring system that evens out talent, and theoretically makes golf enjoyable for everyone. Theoretically.

Or if they wish to send an abusive text to the Cabinet Maker.

12. They are liberal in the sense that they are tolerant of all sorts. They do not preface their political opinions with 'I'm not a racist, me, but …', and they do not refer to their other half as the 'Pleasure Prevention Officer'. Hierarchies make them nervous. Their views are their own, not those of the Daily Mail, The Guardian or that person from Google that they met at their godchild's wedding last weekend.

13. They do not offer unsolicited advice, ever, and they manage to look genuinely shocked when your most recent shot lands in a completely different Ordnance Survey grid square from its intended destination.

14. They do not consider you a functioning alcoholic when you offer them a nip of Jura malt after the 5th, 8th, 11th and 15th. And if they do, they would never say, especially if they are your doctor.

15. They get a move on, and know instinctively when to concede a 'Gimme',[6] and when not to. They appreciate that novice golf is about the mastery of fear, coupled with the management of expectations.

---

[6]Gimme: the tactical concession of a hole when your opponent is close enough to be almost certain of getting the ball in with his next stroke. Remembering that golf is a game played as much in the mind as with the body, a well-deployed, unoffered Gimme is also a fine way of winding up an opponent

16. They have a rich sense of the ridiculous, which is why they are on a golf course in the first place. This also happens with US Presidential hopefuls, it seems.

17. They understand disappointment and can handle it. They have grasped that anticipated collapse of hope hovers in the air of a golf course like a Liberal Democrat manifesto.

18. They laugh, because that is how God differentiated them from the rest of the animal kingdom. And also from Angela Merkel.

*

So there you are, master of all you survey, standing on the raised first tee and looking out at the Elysian setting before you. Rolling parkland stretches out into the deep beyond, punctuated by majestic oaks and perhaps a church spire peeping over a distant hedge. Rooks call noisily from a stand of cedars on the hill, and sheep safely graze in an adjoining field. It is not recognised often enough that mindless optimism plays a large part in the tool kit of the amateur sportsman, and right now, it seems almost inconceivable that you won't give a spectacular display of competence whilst surrounded by all this beauty. Your host has played his first shot (225 yards, slightly left of centre, on the fairway, 'bit disappointed with that'), and now there is the small matter of you doing the same. It is at this exact moment that you come to accept the foolishness of having implied, when he originally issued the invitation, that golf held no terrors for you; it persuaded him that you had talent, and you thereby failed to manage his expectations. Actually, allowing for your non-existent modesty, it persuaded him that you were probably bloody good at it.

There are 381 yards between you and the first pin[7], and around 6200 yards between you and the moment you can hurl your golf bag into the boot of your car in 4 hours' time and return home to kick the Jack Russell. You set the ball on its tee, deliberately too high as the shot you most fear is the head-up topped scuff, and then you do a few practise swings. The first one stubs itself into the ground a couple of feet behind where it should have been, and it is not until the 5th or 6th that you feel ready to 'address the ball'. Your host quietly says 'no hurry', whilst silently wondering if he will be home in time for Newsnight.

You get as far as the backswing, but something terrible happens: in all the self-inflicted pressure you suddenly forget how to play golf. Muscle memory has suddenly been replaced by muscle amnesia and each of the 24000 twitching nerves involved in the shot refer back up to the brain, asking: 'what the hell do I do next?', a question to which your brain has no sensible answer. In his book, *Outliers*, Malcolm Gladwell asserts in his '10,000 hour rule' that this is the amount of practise time a normal

---

[7]The stick with the triangular flag on it that seemingly marks where everyone's ball but yours is headed.

person needs to become world class at something. In terms of actually swinging a club, as opposed to chasing your ball around a course, you have probably played golf for 10-15 hours at most, which leaves you with slightly more than 99.95% left to do, and this is the wrong time to be thinking about it. Your immediate problem is that you simply cannot visualise the club head swinging through in the same geographical vicinity as your static ball, like the book told you it would, and you panic. Instead of leaving nature to look after the next 2 or 3 seconds, you concoct some parody of mechanical action that contrives to go way underneath and to the right hand side of the ball, which subsequently rises high into the air like a startled pheasant.

Call it what you will, and for tasteless reasons that we need not go in to the Cabinet Maker calls it a 'Douglas Bader', your ball is some 23 yards on its way to the distant hole, with 358 yards left to travel. At this rate, you will be going round in a shade under 260; ironically, the same number of shots as Jason Day needed for his record-breaking full 4 rounds of the 2015 PGA Championship. The unfair thing is that even to get that far, your ball has actually covered about 100 yards in the vertical dimension.

Smiles are wearing that little bit thinner already. It is going to be a long afternoon.

*

Let us draw a discreet veil over this imaginary round for a moment and dip in to examine some of what is in that bag of yours, apart from the catering pack of Mini Twix and hip flask of sloe gin, of course, and work out what it is supposed to do. We need to do this at an early stage as that bag is going to play a quite unreasonably large part in your life from now on. You are going to depend on it and hate it in equal measure, and you will allocate blame to its contents with a ferocity that you never realised you could muster. Occasionally, you will angrily strew those contents around the local countryside, and then apologise to those who have been watching you do so. Very rarely will you feel any affection for it. Once the dopamine high of initially buying it has subsided, it will have exactly the same role in your life as that ex-girlfriend who still manages to mention your shortcomings to public amusement every time you bump into her.

The bag's primary function is to enable you to transport the tools of your trade, in this case golf, around the workplace. The rules of the game allow you to carry no more than 14 clubs, each one of which is theoretically designed to allow you to do something slightly different from the others, and these form the bulk of what you carry around. You also carry a sufficient stock of small, normally white, balls to get you round 4 miles of countryside without running out, plus some tees to enable you to elevate your ball at the beginning of each hole, an action that theoretically makes it easier to hit it more powerfully towards its destination.

For the beginner, that is a sufficient cargo. The enthusiast might also add a towel, a ground repair tool, gloves, ball markers, and club head covers, as presumably this will allow him and her to get some basic laundry and DIY in during the round. The professional, who we should note doesn't actually have to carry his clubs himself, will also have a distance finder, a golf organiser and a whole range of kit that the company that is sponsoring him would like the rest of us be inspired to buy. The Undergraduate, known to his golfing friends as the Diviner owing to his uncanny knack of finding water, also carries an old shrimping net.

Back in the day, club-heads, such as they were, were made out of a tough wood like holly, hickory or pear, whilst the shafts were made out of ash or hazel. There were long-noses, spoons, niblicks and cleeks in place of todays' woods, irons, wedges and putters, and the ball was made out of heavily compressed feathers. It is not entirely clear who played the game back then, excepting that the sheer cost of the equipment would have limited it to the rich.

From my own point of view, I found for many years that I normally only needed around 5 clubs. A 3 wood to see the ball merrily on its way; a hybrid[8] to push it along the middle bit; a 9 iron to chip it onto the green; a sand wedge

---

[8] A Hybrid is what happens when a wooden club mates with an iron one.

in case of unpleasantness in a bunker, and a putter to plonk it in the hole. I can see that you might think, on a casual read, that I needed just 5 shots to get down that last hole. You are wrong. In this example, I used both the hybrid and the putter 3 times each, which meant I was down in 9. Depending on who you are, this bit of information has either made you feel superior, or amongst friends. The accumulated calories that I must have expended carrying around clubs that I will never use, clubs whose function remain a complete mystery to me, would feed an army. To my certain knowledge, there was a 4 iron in my bag that had never left it when it eventually went to the knackers' yard. Many clubs had been there so long that the gum on their handles had melted them together, and simultaneously to the side of the bag. I couldn't remove them if I wanted to. They are fated to remain there, in someone else's possession, until they get a congratulatory telegram from the reigning monarch in about 65 years time.

Proper players, however, have proper kit, and they use it all. Slightly less, it has to be said, than they talk about it. It is not for nothing that the global golf industry is worth an annual $70 billion, equivalent to the GDP of Burma and Jamaica combined, or that the market capitalisation of Callaway – just one brand in a forest of golfing brands – for example, is close to $900 million. In the UK, the average golfer spends £2486 a year on their game (2011), of which £72 goes on balls alone. I love that- £72 a year on golf balls[9]! In my experience, you can always tell someone who pays £2486 a year on their golf by watching them protecting their clubs between shots with a bewildering array of woolly cosies and hats; not forgetting their dire habit of banging on endlessly about how their magnificent drive opened up the eighth green that afternoon, long after their other half has gone to bed with the postman.

And the *leitmotif* of their game happens to be the driver.

For the average alpha male golfer, in stark contrast to me, modern history began in 1990 when Callaway introduced the steel-headed Big Bertha, and ended 22 years later when the TaylorMade R1 Driver provided him with 12 different lofts and 7 different face angles, none of which he had the faintest idea what to do with. For males, at least, these developments allow precious hours absence from any disappointment they might feel over the size of their penises, and even more precious hours identifying local flora and fauna as they crawl around the woods retrieving drives that have gone 180 yards at right angles to the tee. Just because Ernie Els can regularly ease a ball 290 yards down the fairway at will does not, I regret, mean

---

[9]If you spend a lot of time in the rough, you will lose balls. Fact. If you spend all your time on the fairway, you will never find other people's lost balls. However, if you always walk through the rough on your way from tee to green, irrespective of whether you put a ball there, you will keep finding lost balls, and nearly always end your round in profit.

that the rest of us can. You can say 'drive for show, putt for dough' as often as you like, but there will always be someone in your group whose principal mission in a round is to pulverise his ball into the neighbouring county, on the basis that once in every eighteen holes it will work and everyone else will say 'yee-haa', or something similarly encouraging. In our group this service is provided by the Undergraduate. Personally, I resist the temptation to use a driver just as I resist recreational drugs, by saying 'no'. I do not possess the required maturity to deal with the responsibility required, and have given mine to the British Heart Foundation shop in Midhurst. Ironically, they had it on sale for £10, which is exactly what I had paid the Cancer Research shop for it a year or so earlier which, if nothing else, tells you something about the velocity of money supply in a post-inflationary world.

For the last 10 years or so, the hybrid club has taken the place of some lower numbered woods and irons by providing the best of both for decent players once they make it onto the fairway. Speaking for myself, I could quite easily have got from tee to green without ever getting onto the fairway, but I acknowledge that I may have been in a minority here. The adept golfer will want to boost his extravagant drive by going as far as he can towards the hole without teeing up to do so, which he is not allowed to do, unless absolutely no one is watching. Thus, for your average Graham, who is out on the course relaxing from his taxi driving as many as 14 times a week, a hybrid gives him the length provided by a wood, at the same time as the swing mechanics of an iron. It doesn't give him friends, or people to play with, but that is another matter altogether which you will probably have to take up with his mother. Research has taught me that the loft provided by a hybrid is anywhere between 16 and 55 degrees, which is both instructive and confusing to someone who still thinks a loft is where you keep teenage copies of *Health and Efficiency*. The Banker has a ruinously expensive hybrid in his bag and we find that it furnishes him simultaneously with the hideous inaccuracy of a low wood, and the pathetic distance of a high iron. Coming as he does from an industry that dragged the rest of us to within an ace of financial oblivion less than 10 years ago, he consoles himself with muttered bits of client advice and an offer to himself of the cheapest gap insurance in town.

Which brings us to the Pitching Wedge, in my humble opinion the supreme criterion that divides decent golfers from people like me. Wikipedia has it down as 'a versatile club on the cusp of high irons and wedges,' there to provide a high trajectory shot when something evil has got between you and the flag. Your average Margaret, who hopes to be Lady's Captain in 4 years' time, will routinely deploy this club to great effect from around 80-100 yards, and when there are things like hedges, bunkers or fish in the way; it provides her with glorious highs on the way in, and back-spin on arrival, unlike her husband, who clearly doesn't. The Cabinet Maker recently emerged triumphantly from yet another visit to World of Golf in New Malden with a Lofted Wedge still in its wrapper, and confident enough to put a substantial wager on the outcome of the next hour or so. Suffice it to say that the Wedge on its own added 12 strokes to his round and it is currently available (£3.99) alongside my driver at the British Heart Foundation shop in Midhurst. That's the thing about golf: it parts a fool and his money quicker than you can get Sarah Palin to say something dumb and offensive. But the Cabinet Maker will get over it soon enough once he has seen it all through the comforting prism of class struggle.

*

The reader will have got the point by now, long before we have had to complete our fictional round, and the point is that we are very, very early in a career that could go one of two very different ways.

The first of these ways is the right one, the one we aim for. It is what Prospero described as being 'of such stuff as dreams are made on'. In this version, we play a couple of experimental rounds and take our first lesson. Having flattered us outrageously – ('a natural swing, if I might say so, Sir; one of the best I've seen on a beginner'), the pro sets about building a solid platform on which our future game may be built. We learn to lean slightly forward, to bend our knees, to put our chin up and to swing the club head gently through the ball, generating sufficient speed to power the ball in roughly the direction we intended.

We practise once or twice a week, and take enough lessons to ensure no bad habits creep in. Our confidence rises at the same rate as our scores fall, and we begin to talk about it all rather more than polite society would like us to. We get a few qualifying rounds in, and play a competition or two, before the pro takes us round the course himself and signs off our handicap certificate. We are now ready to take our game round the world and add our little bit to the $70 billion already being invested each year.

The second of these ways is the one we fear, and we fear it because we sense its inevitability. It has sat, vulture like, on our shoulders these last thirty years, and it knows us too well to flap away now. Our lack of previous sporting excellence happens, annoyingly, to be the best predictor as to what will follow in every new sport that we apply ourselves to. If you do what you've always done, you'll get what you always got, and all that. We plough remorselessly on, decade after decade, course after course, never shaking off the ghastly habits we were born with, and fated never to break the magical 100, let alone get a handicap. Research tells us that only 29% of adult golfers ever shoot a round in below 100 shots, which reduces to 21% and 5% for 90 and 80 respectively, so we needed to be within the top third of golfers in the country just to achieve what we had initially set out to do.

This second category of golfers risk becoming part of that small unhappy tribe who only ever get invited for a round once by any one person, and consequently have to have the widest possible circle of friends. Our answer to the question 'are you a golfer?' is at the same time honest and deliberately misleading. 'I have my moments', we say. We are the ones who finish each round with a dignified walk to the private consolation provided by our car, rather than the boastful strut to the Clubhouse Bar. We are the Nearly Men.

Which begins to explain how it was that The Banker, the Cabinet Maker, the Undergraduate and I had arrived at this launch pad. We drained the last of our beer and shuffled out of the Duke of Cumberland towards our destiny.

There was work to be done.

Chapter 3

THE ROAD TO HELL

'It's a funny thing. The more I practise, the luckier I get'.
Arnold Palmer

Not that he ever came clean about it, but it was the Cabinet Maker who cracked first.

I was queueing at a supermarket check-out on the way back from work a week or so after the trial journey to the driving range, when the Professional from the club saw me and wandered over.

'How are you getting on with your golf?' he asked, and after I told him: 'You should book in for a lesson or two, just to get into good habits.'

My father had sent me off for 'a lesson or two' forty years earlier, before this Pro was even born and, for all the use they were to me, they might as well have been delivered by the London School of Tropical Medicine. My uncoordinated teenage body was still trying to cope with A Levels and alcohol consumption, so the chances of it being able to deal effectively with a sport involving no less than 17 different muscle groups were around zero. Besides, my father hadn't actually asked me if I wanted to learn the sport, which I still reckoned to be populated by odd men in checked trousers and appalling polo necked sweaters. I was more interested in controlling my acne, and saving up for the £1.25 that it would cost to buy Fleetwood Mac's *Rumours*. Added to that, I had been given various informal lessons over the years by opponents who were apparently tiring of winning each hole by 2 or 3 strokes, and wanted to put something back into the community by passing on their received wisdom to me. These, too, were as much use as a seminar on morality by any given mayor of London.

By far the best lesson I had ever had was by an anonymous African caddy on a hill top course in Zimbabwe called Nyanga, just about the time that Mozambican guerrillas had stopped planting ambushes and land mines in the surrounding countryside. Each time my ball landed somewhere out in the open, and others were watching, he would not let me play the next shot until he sensed that I was relaxed and ready. But when it landed, as it often did, down in the hidden bits where the lethal wildlife lurked and no one else could see, he would wordlessly grab a club off me and pull off a series of outstanding recovery shots. 25 years later, no round of golf passes without my wishing he hadn't come back to England with me.

'You'd enjoy it,' continued the Pro. 'Just like the Cabinet Maker did earlier this week'

'What? He's started taking lessons with you?' For some irrational reason, this felt like a complete betrayal of the other three, as if he had inserted a dagger between the collective shoulder blades of the team. How could he have done this without telling us he was going to? Lessons were never in the original plan. Taking lessons risked deconstructing the entire idea behind us not being like the others. It smacked of practising, which we'd all agreed was out of bounds.

'Was he any good?' I asked, 'or completely shite? You can be honest with me. He'd expect you to be'.

'Quite impressive, actually,' he said with a slight sniff, and headed out to the car park with his six pack of San Miguel and grab-bag of BBQ flavoured cheesy nibbles.

*

One of the reasons that golf is so difficult to be good at is that there are so many things that can go wrong. Other sports have a lesser margin for error. Rugby, for example, is about the application of brute strength, acceleration and ball handling, and there's not much beyond that. In cycling, the only things that can really go wrong are that you get a puncture at a critical point, or your coach feeds you the wrong concentration of performance enhancing

Erythropoietin. In professional football, you could stub your toe on the ball or use an unsatisfactory brand of hair gel before a key match, but otherwise it is all pretty straightforward. Whereas in golf, the whole edifice that is your game is never more than a single step away from sporting Armageddon.

Everything in golf hangs on the swing: the process of swinging at a stationary ball with the club. Uniquely in a life that had been dedicated to knowing as little as possible about anything I was trying to do, even I realised that I needed to understand it. Whilst in theory it was rather cool to just turn up on the day and play, we very quickly learned that it was extremely un-cool to thrash around in an incompetent haze, delaying the players behind, so it was tacitly agreed that we would try to learn it properly. Even the Undergraduate entered 'swinging' into the Youtube search bar, only to be surprised by some of the strange areas of human endeavour that this led him to.

Amazon has a choice of 1195 books available to you if you wish to learn how to play golf by reading about it and it is comforting to know that, even if you bought and studied every single one of them, you would almost certainly be no better at golf, and Amazon's UK tax bill would probably be no higher either. A compression of all 1195 of them into a single paragraph would look something like this:

There are 2 types of golfer – swingers (who use centrifugal

force) and hitters (who use centripetal force), employing 17 different muscle groups to produce 5 different shots (drive, approach, pitch, wedge and putt) in 4 distinct phases (take-off, upswing, downswing and follow through) to manoeuvre the ball from tee to hole. For the 13 things that can go wrong with the shot generated by one of 14 possible clubs (slice, hook, push, pull, top, toe, heel, fat, thin, pop-up, whiff, shank or drop-kick) there are 16 cures. These include rotation, shifting, closing the face, putting the right shoulder back, lining the left hip over the ball, swinging from the inside, flattening the left wrist, strengthening the grip and transferring weight appropriately, but not all at the same time. Really clever golfers can deliberately draw or fade a ball to the left or right respectively around an obstacle. Every now and again, you may hit a shot that does and goes precisely what and where it was designed to do and go, a 'pure', but I see we may be getting some distance ahead of ourselves.

A second paragraph might run to some discussion on the invisible mental battles involved. Just as every sound golfer visualises his next shot doing precisely what he has designed it to do, people like me just dream of it ending up nearer the hole than it started. Rory McIlroy presumably mentally breaks down a hole of 570 yards into a) a huge drive that fades ever so slightly around that protruding birch tree, b) a sweet approach shot, c) a chip to within 4 foot of the pin and d) a rattling birdie putt that has the crowd in raptures. Faced with the same hole, unlikely though that eventuality may seem, the Cabinet Maker would start by dividing 570 by the 80 or so yards he was confident of hitting each shot, making 7. He would then allow a further 3 to get around said birch tree having lodged his ball in the folds of one of its roots, 2 more when his ball went out of bounds onto the footpath by that cross lady's bicycle, and finally 4 putting the 16 footer once on the green, ending up with a nice 16. 'Out here', as Mike Weir said, 'it's just you and the ball'. Or, in the case of the Undergraduate, just you, the ball and whichever of your 862 friends you happen to be Snap-chatting or Insta-gramming at the time.

'Loss,' says elite performance coach Michelle Cleere, 'is feedback', which suggests that most of us have had a great deal of feedback in our sporting careers. In the last forty years, I have had more of this feedback than most, and have come to the rather clumsy conclusion that loss is nature's way of telling me to drink more beer. I went to a prep school that was so catastrophically awful at sport that the Headmaster began each term with a short lecture about the importance of being a good loser – long before we had played the first of our matches. The notion of possible victory simply hadn't occurred to him, and I imagine he thought it would be irresponsible preparing us for something that was probably never going to happen. He probably subscribed to the paradox of Genghis Khan's hawk, in which what you think you most desire is actually the thing that you least need, or something along those lines. This inculcated in me an unhealthily cheerful acceptance of being on the losing side so long as the opponent wasn't a crowing git, a banker, or an Australian.

What the Cabinet Maker had been persuaded to spend £30 a session on, (and, let's face it, we all sooner or later decided to do as well), was the construction of a solid platform from which relatively consistent shots could be played. That way, he explained lamely once it had become apparent that he had been rumbled, he could play through the lengthy periods of poor form that would punctuate his otherwise feeble efforts. Because, besides being a scheming charlatan, the Cabinet Maker was in fact articulating a need as old as time and as basic as the requirement for food, water, safety and Maltesers. He had arrived at that particular age where a body awakes one morning and realises that it has less days to live than it has already lived, and is entering into a zone of actuarial uncertainty. And, although the four of us come from the British tribe that publicly celebrates rank amateurism and finds virtue in mediocrity, there comes a time in everyone's life when a man just wants to be OK at something. Not good, you will understand, but a long way less than awful.

For me, this feeling was well reflected by a memorial bench on the 3rd tee that celebrates the life of an old member as merely being 'liked by everyone'. Part of what our group was about was the wish to amount to something more than a park bench. In fact, one of the abiding terrors of my life has been the notion that someone will shove a bench with my name on it on some local beauty spot before I am cold in the clay, and then apply some vacuous monogram on it to the effect that I 'meant well'. If a park bench turned out to be all that my golf had ever amounted to, I wanted it to say something like: 'Roger. Master of the Eagles', which would at least leave plenty of room for idle speculation. Besides, we were uncertain as a group if we were liked by anyone, let alone everyone.

Where the Cabinet Maker had merely been underhand, the Banker was downright dishonest. Having the luxury of a job that involved copious travelling around the country, he had quietly checked himself into a leading, distant and probably ruinously expensive, golf school for some serious lessons. It is easy to imagine the scene. Somewhere in the heart of St George's Hill, among the social ambition, the Audis and the azaleas, a deferential Pro speaking in hushed and admiring tones of the Banker's 'natural posture' and 'purist's swing', whilst privately cursing the day that he had finally failed to make it onto the European tour, and had to spend a career doing this kind of thing instead. Then the settling of the account in the shop where everything cost twice what it did at Southdowns, and three times the equivalent at American Golf. 'A swing like yours, Sir, if I may say so, deserves the very best of clubs, and if I might humbly suggest this set of Mizuno JPX 850 graphite irons … what's that, Sir? The cost? You're particularly fortunate, Sir, as they are down from £600 to £504 per club today.'

And thus the Master of the Universe climbs back into his BMW for the long journey home, but not before mildly scuffing each club in the grit of the car park so that he can announce them to his cynical friends as being second hand.

I complained about all this to the Artist that evening, and her response surprised me. She had an honorary doctorate in coping with the rise and falls of my various enthusiasms over the years, and she had every right to assume that this was but another of them. But she didn't. She suggested that I would be better, and therefore happier, if I allowed someone to teach me the rudiments of the swing, and that I might actually enjoy it all more, and for longer, if I made a small investment in getting better at it.

The following morning, I closed my office door and made my own furtive call to the Pro. I was anxious not to be overheard doing so, partly because I was paid to work, not to make dubious calls, and partly because I had the dawning realisation of how a man must feel when he first books in to the 'social' diseases clinic. The Pro was out on the course, and I duly left a message for him to call back. When he did so, he went through to the main switchboard, with the effect that my guilty little secret became public knowledge.

'Sorry I didn't take your call first time,' he said. 'I was out on the driving range with your son. A hell of a drive he's got, I'd say.' This was Kim Philby to the Cabinet Maker's Guy Burgess.

'Who paid for that, might I ask?'

'His grandmother.'

There were traitors everywhere.

*

Thus the process of initiation ground on.

Motivated by the need to get one back on the fun-sponge Secretary down in Cornwall, just as much as by the search for excellence, we all took a number of lessons (2, 3, 3 and 37 for the Undergraduate, me, the Cabinet Maker and the Banker respectively). Then we all started to search out the equipment we needed, albeit in very different ways.

The matter of selecting golf equipment is a complex one, sandwiched as it is between the law of diminishing returns and its friend, the law of diminishing marginal utility. The first of these laws states that if you change one factor (the club) and keep the other factors (you) constant, you will get a lessening return on each increment of your investment. The second of these states that your satisfaction and benefit will fail to increase in tandem with the rising inputs (equipment). We Benthamites take it a stage further, by equating usefulness with the increase of pleasure and the avoidance of pain, but we may be running ahead of ourselves again. Swapping sciences, the entire golfing industry is predicated upon idiots firing up their own dopamine neurotransmitters when they see a box of Titleist Pro V1 at £4.50 per ball, when they would achieve just as much by spending £1.00 for one of those recovered balls that every Pro's shop keeps in a wicker basket next to the outsize ladies' trousers.

For the Undergraduate, equipment was straightforward: he had no clubs and therefore had to get some. Equally, he had no money and therefore had to a) find some very cheap ones and b) persuade someone in his family that this was a justifiable capital cost, and not going to be spent on beer or Jello Shots, that would in turn just be pissed up against the wall. In the end, he found a complete new set for £149 which was, ironically, the same figure that the Banker had paid for his left shoe. And the annoying thing about a bag of 14 clubs at £149 is that, in the right hands, they are almost as good as the personally fitted £2500 Taylor Made specials. 'In the right hands'. That is the key. The Undergraduate was a smart enough student of Business Management to understand that there was no point on God's earth in him having expensive clubs until he could optimise what he could do with the cheap ones. So he then spent three hours on the driving range, concentrating exclusively on one club (the driver) and one aim (300 yards), before announcing to the others that he felt good and ready for a competitive round. It is a compelling feature of the Undergraduate's golf that he seems to feel that the short game[10] is something that only happens to other people.

I was in a slightly different situation in that I had made a rather too early, and rather too public, virtue of the age of my bag of clubs, and of how only complete dicks bought fancy new equipment before they had mastered any given sport.

'I will buy new clubs,' I said with ridiculous gravitas, 'once I have got round a course in under 100. Because then and only then will I know that I have a proper swing'. It was a golfing version of self-immolation, akin to David Cameron calling a referendum on UK's membership of the EU just because he hadn't got anything better to say on that particular evening, and because he wanted to appeal to someone called Mavis in Southend. It was not so much creating a hostage to fortune, as being utterly illogical.

'Tosser,' said the Cabinet Maker. 'You'll buy new clubs when you get pissed off with your current ones being laughed at every time you set foot on a course. It will be nothing to do with the golf. Or when you get told to by the Pro, because you're unteachable.'

---

[10]The short game is the bit that takes place near the green, where violence and power give way to precision and delicacy. Unless you are the Undergraduate.

He had a point. They were forty years old and, other than to their owner, they looked like something that one might hire in a theatrical costume shop when one's local Amateur Drama group were doing a Jeeves and Wooster special. Next door to the Undergraduate's cheap and cheerful set, let alone the Banker's diamante-encrusted Virginia Water specials, mine had the hopeless air of a Labour Party activist in Chichester. The irons were thin and anaemic alongside today's chunky wedges, the woods were unfeasibly small, and the putter just looked as if someone had substituted it for a real one by way of an April Fool. The bag itself had seen better days half a century before, and now appeared to have reached that stage in its deterioration when a trip to Dignitas beckoned and was surely the kindest thing. Even the Artist was offering to buy me a new set if this all turned out to be more than a passing fad.

The Pro was actually quite kind about them when I finally got up to the driving range for my first lesson, but then he had a long-term financial reason to be.

'Let's start with an 8 iron,' he said, 'and take it from there'.

This was easier said than done, as the 8 iron was hermetically sealed by its handle to its friend four numbers lower down, and wasn't going anywhere. I gave it a few gentle tugs, but it started coming apart from its own handle.

'I think I'm a bit of a 6 iron man myself,' I lied. 'Shall we start with that?'

I steadied myself for my first stroke, suddenly feeling too tall to be dealing with the small white ball on the matting in front of me, too stiff to be swinging freely, and too old to be hitting anything remotely hard. But, in the event, like the knee that miraculously loses its pain when finally taken to the doctor, I struck the ball sweetly enough, and it headed down the range in an encouraging arc. There were two different dramas playing out; I had played a shot way better than I had any right to have expected, at the same time as playing a shot that confirmed all the Pro's most pessimistic fears about the raw material he was dealing with.

'That was probably crap,' I offered, fishing for a compliment in the time-honoured fashion.

'Oh, I wouldn't go that far,' he said. 'You should see *some* of the beginners that I get up here'

And there it was in a nutshell. Even though I had thrashed around golf courses on and off for over forty years, and played the game on 71 different courses in 14 different countries and 4 continents, I had still managed to sell myself to the Pro on the basis of one shot, and not even a particularly shabby shot at that, as a complete beginner. Ten years earlier, I might have been slightly offended, but not now. Now, I was mildly amused and very encouraged. At the age of 56, I had just discovered the golfing equivalent of clocking a used car, and I wasn't about to correct the misunderstanding.

*

Whilst the four of us went about our preparations for a year of golf in our different ways, it was the Undergraduate who broke cover first with a proper game.

One Friday morning, he kicked his younger brother out of bed and took him to Southdowns for what he fondly believed would be a full eighteen holes. Where the Undergraduate was confident and cocky by nature, the Student was more deliberate and self-effacing, which promised from an early stage to lead to an interesting fusion of styles.

The wise move, in view of their inexperience and propensity to mess up the simplest of shots, might have been to start their round an hour or so before dusk, far from the public gaze and with only a minimal risk of annoying an easily riled club member. Rule 1 in the world of beginners' golf, after all, is to avoid attracting attention at all costs, although this was not how the Undergraduate saw things:

'It's our club, and we can play who we like, when we like,' he had announced. 'They'll be delighted to see us and to know that their course is being properly utilised.' So saying, he had booked a start time at 8.30 a.m, the club's equivalent of gridlock. 8.30 a.m is the time of day when retired people, who have been wide awake since 5.15 worrying about the decline in manners and immigration, take to the golf courses of England in their swarms.

Rule 2 is to bring a bag of clubs each, rather than assume that the other members will welcome the sight of 2 young men sharing out of the same bag. Research never played a large part in the Undergraduate's routines, and this small requirement had clean passed him by. The Pro was kind and let them in, making the point that it would be nice to see them both with bags next time out.

Rule 3 is to avoid future trouble by waving through anyone who looks as though they can play the game, and specifically anyone, male or female, with a moustache. This is particularly important on the first tee, where everything is depressingly public, and where proceedings tend to be observed by elderly people waiting frigidly for their own start times, with all the allure of the prospect of a long weekend in Woking.

'Shall we just get out of your way and crack on in front of you?' asked a moustache that was a quarter of a foursome of elderly gentlemen that had booked the start time immediately after them. Loosely translated, this might more accurately read: '*Your sin is your youth. Please get out of our way.'* He then added, enigmatically: 'It's normally easier'.

The Undergraduate waved them through, only then to watch them go through a lengthy performance of calisthenics and practise swings that lasted until their real start time, and ensured that the next pairing had arrived and would be breathing down their necks for the remainder of the round. There are some human groupings whose sheer unreasonableness allows, demands even, recreational drug use.

As soon as the foursome had disappeared down the fairway, the Undergraduate hopped onto the raised tee and prepared for his shot.

'I'd give them another few minutes', suggested the Student, watching the foursome lining up their approach shots.

But he didn't. Attention deficit is a fickle companion at the best of times, but on a golf course it can be fatal.

'They'll be fine,' he said confidently. 'They're nearly on the green'.

Rule 4 is simple. It dictates that, should you play a shot before the players in front have disappeared from view, or are 300 yards or more down the course, you will play the most violently successful shot of your life.

This shot will land just behind them and then chortle merrily up past their assembled trolleys and footwear, before coming to a very public rest alongside one of their balls. This would not be considered good form by the most genial golfer on earth, far less so by a group of dinosaurs already in deep mourning at the passing of the age of deference. More importantly, it surrenders any of the moral high ground that might have been gained by waving them through in the first place. Besides, it places a tiresome moral qualification on the enjoyment of a rare good stroke.

The Undergraduate offered futile apologies by way of hand signals, shrugs and words that the gentlemen in front were too blind to see, too deaf to hear and too cross to deal with.

'You should have waited,' added one of the lemon-faced women waiting behind them.

In philosophical terms, the Undergraduate's golf mirrors the Dichotomy Paradox, (Rule 5 for beginners,) whereby to go anywhere (eg the hole) you will first go half the distance (eg the drive), then half the remainder of the distance, then half again and so on until you reach infinity. Zeno the Greek, of course, used this paradox to prove that the universe is singular, that change, including motion, is impossible, and that the Undergraduate's putting is diabolical.

The developing problem for the two of them at this stage was around 200 yards to their immediate South and closing fast. (Rule 6, by the way, is that if you tangle with a pair of female players in hats, and pushing huge trolleys with short, hurried and slightly constipated steps, you are going to come off second best. Every time.) The Student and the Undergraduate were waiting for the elderly men to finish putting out on the first green, which seemed to be taking an age, whilst becoming nervously aware of a double dose of Waitrose-nurtured fury stomping down the hill behind them. They were caught in a trap, and not even one of their own making, and all the cheerful politeness of two relatively civilised young men was going to get them precisely nowhere.

The denouement was reached after the younger pair had putted out on the first green. The smaller of the two ladies following them headed them off as they made their way to the second tee.

'Are you new here?' she asked.

'Yes. It's our first round. My name's Tom,' and he held his right hand out in greeting.

She ignored it.

'Let me give you a bit of advice, young man' she said. 'This is a busy time of day on a busy golf course, and people of your standard would be much better off respecting that, and playing at other times.' Her cap quivered slightly as she spoke, giving her the air of some old American cartoon character.

The Student pointed at the elderly quartet in front, still faffing around on the second tee with their woolly club cosies and monogrammed balls.

'I'm really sorry if we're holding you up,' he said, 'but we're being held up ourselves'.

'That is really of no interest to us,' said her larger friend, who had caught up. 'In my opinion, you are simply not of the required standard for a busy course. That's all. I shall make my views known to the Professional when I get back in.' She had the practised air of someone who made her views on virtually everything known far and wide, and on a very regular basis. If a copy of the *Daily Mail* wasn't actually in her bag, it was most certainly on the front seat of her car, presumably open on the letters page. Her husband was probably drowning himself at that very moment.

'Are you asking us to leave the course?' asked the Undergraduate

'I think it's for the best, don't you?' replied the fat one, smiling thinly.

'Though nothing personal implied, you do understand,' said the thin one, smiling fatly.

For all the criticism normally aimed at the manners of teenagers and young men, the Undergraduate and the Student were too stunned to make anything in the way of a come-back, partly because they were well aware that there was a year of paid membership to get through and these were early days. Rule 8, after all, is that the clever thing you just said in the heat of the moment will become the best speech you ever regretted. They collected up their bits and pieces and walked back along an adjacent footpath to the club house.

'Why didn't you tell them to fuck off?' asked the Student.

'Simple. I didn't want to embarrass you.'

As Jean-Paul Sartre once irritatingly said: 'freedom is what you do with what's been done to you.'[11]

---

[11]He also said that 'life begins on the other side of despair', which probably goes a long way to explaining how we got through the first few months.

Chapter 4

DEAD CATS AND CONDOMS

'No plan survives contact with the enemy'
Helmuth von Moltke

'Everyone has a plan until they get punched in the mouth'
Mike Tyson

Not that I would necessarily know, but initially it felt much like trying to buy pornography as a teenage boy.

Despair at the disparity between my skill level (low and sinking fast) and those of my colleagues (suspiciously improving) had persuaded me that their lowest common denominator was new equipment and that I needed to address this deficit urgently. Which case of affairs indirectly led me to shuffle anonymously into the Hedge End branch of American Golf one Monday lunchtime in April. It wasn't the sort of thing you necessarily told your friends that you were doing, but it had to be done, a kind of Schrodinger's Cat scenario where you were both there, and not there, simultaneously. Without the gunpowder or quantum mechanics, obviously. Or the hydrocyanic acid, or Geiger Counter. Or the steel chamber. Or the cat, come to think of it.

I parked my car discreetly outside Toolstation, and then sidled furtively in to American Golf when I was confident that no one I knew would be there. Having banged on endlessly about how virtuous my old set of clubs made me, it was something of a betrayal to go and buy new ones, and I needed to reveal my change of heart at a time of my own choosing, not someone elses'.

'Can anyone here tell me about golf clubs?' I asked at the counter. It was a question that deserved contempt, and duly received it.

'What sort of club are you after?'

'Something that makes me brilliant'

The young Sales Assistant sized me up, and we walked past serried ranks of clubs on the wall, each one of which looked as though it would do wonders for my game. There were some that I had heard of, like Callaway and Ping, and many others that I hadn't, from Cobra through Fazer to Mizuno, and way beyond. Everywhere I looked there were toys: things that I was aware of like gloves, tees and practise balls, right through to things that I had absolutely no previous knowledge of, like the TruSwing Golf Swing Sensor (£349.99), and the positively adorable SkyCaddie

SkyPro Swing Analyser Training Aid (£149.99). How the hell had I survived two or three months of proper golf without the help of this stuff?

It seemed to me that the naysayers and advertising men had been right all along. How you applied yourself to gaining the necessary skills counted for almost nothing. The more money you spent on this game the better you would get. It was as simple as that.

He led me into a mini driving range and he then handed me a standard club, suggesting that he should 'have a quick look at my swing'. It was exactly what I had hoped he wouldn't want a quick look at. As far as I was concerned he was welcome to take a quick look at my cholesterol levels, my bank balance or my voting record even, but I really didn't want him looking at my swing. I just wanted him to ask me how much I could afford to spend and to convince me that this would dictate how good I could subsequently become at golf. My swing was irrelevant, a strictly personal matter, and the way I saw it, it should have no bearing at all on my ability at golf. Besides, mine was a swing that regularly had people falling about with laughter on neighbouring fairways, and I was not overkeen on revealing it in a warehouse full of taxi drivers in Nike Classic Polo shirts.

I swung, and the ball lurched violently off into some canvas sheeting on the right. The salesman said nothing, but immediately produced a different and pricier club for me try, insinuating that my incompetence had nothing to do with it. I swung again, and it went slightly better. He purred appreciatively, and handed me another club, another 10% more expensive. This piece of Vaudeville continued for some time until, eventually, I had a spectacularly expensive Japanese club in my hands. I swung for a sixth time and the ball flew straight and true. We turned round to look at the monitoring screen and watched the yardage unfold: 150, 160,170, 180, … 188. I had just hit a golf ball 188 yards with a 6 iron.

'That,' he said gravely, 'was a wonderful golf shot'. The clouds had parted, and I was born again. There was no going back.

'How much?' I asked rather too quickly. A result like this needed to be bottled immediately, like a good dessert wine. The dopamine neurotransmitters were in overdrive and I wanted to have those clubs in my car before someone else grabbed them. With those little beauties in my possession I would never look back.

To my surprise, he named a figure that was well within my budget, adding that I was fortunate to have chosen today to be in there as they had their unrepeatable, today-only, 1% off promotion on until 8.00 pm that evening. It was only when we got to the counter that he and I realised simultaneously that what he was *transmitting* was 'price per club', and that what I was *receiving* was 'price for full set of 14 clubs + bag + woolly club-head protectors thrown in for good measure'. My total budget was in the very low hundreds, whilst his price for the set was, to the penny, what my parents had paid for their first house.

'That will be exactly £1800,' he had said, 'and I'll throw in some club-head protectors for you'. He didn't even look embarrassed.

Twenty minutes later, our relationship not being quite as cordial as it had been at the £1800 level, I left the premises with six new irons, a 3 wood and a hybrid, all from their standard promotional range. I shut the boot, and texted the others:

'I'm unstoppable. You are officially too scared to play me any more. Gits.'

I might have bought the cheaper clubs, but their mere presence in the back of the car made me feel that another Rubicon had been crossed in my long journey.

*

We had come to the conclusion that we needed to start our serious golf at a basic course, and work our way up. Somewhere with almost no obstacles, and well used to people like us.

Somehow we knew that we had to benchmark how far we had come and how far we had to go, but also we had to do so amongst people who didn't necessarily populate the local Rotary Clubs and didn't aspire to climb up the greasy pole of golf club hierarchy until that golden faraway dawn that someone whispered in their ear that they were going to be Captain in four years' time.

By searching 'worst golf club in the UK' on Tripadvisor, we created a short list of 6 possible candidates: one in Inner London, 2 in Essex, 1 in Liverpool, one in North Yorkshire and one in South Wales. The relative merits and demerits of each were exhaustively discussed before we opted for the most local of the list, an inner city municipal pay-and-play in South West London, somewhere between the River Wandle and a block of streets where someone the Undergraduate had once fancied now lived. As always with Tripadvisor it was difficult to work out who was being fair and who was just getting their own back, but we had to start somewhere.

We knew little or nothing of the course but, for a reason that seemed sensible enough at the time, like the fact that his petrol was paid for by his employers, we felt that it was a good idea to arrive in £60K of the Banker's German metalware.

At first glance, I thought we had arrived in a car wash depot, as opposed to a golf club. A high percentage of the car park was coned off as if it was part of a recent crime scene. There was water spraying out of power hoses everywhere you looked. Two Poles were energetically scrubbing a Romanian plated Volkswagen on one side of our car, whilst a man who introduced himself as Abdul was hosing down a Mitsubishi on the other. He offered his services which, judging by the Banker's reaction, looked as though they included protecting the car for us whilst we were out on the course and getting hold of some prescription painkillers for us for our return. The Undergraduate subordinated his middle class home counties accent into something that sounded like, 'No tanks bro', which impressed the rest of us mightily, but just left Abdul looking confused and a little depressed.

To call the building we went to a Clubhouse would be stretching things, but we went along to settle up for our round anyway. It had the feel of something that had been prefabricated many years before for a short term job that had never really been completed and was now confused about its central purpose. Two gentlemen walked past us dressed in hi-visibility jackets, collected their clubs from the rack outside, left their hard hats on the back of their pick-up, and headed for the first tee. The club's one rule ('No play in Overalls, please') was displayed above the head of the friendly Pro, who asked us for £7.50 each.

The Banker, spotting possibly the smallest bill he had seen in his adult life as an opportunity not to appear as tight as usual, theatrically exclaimed that it was all 'on him', that we would be his guests for the round, and would we each like a Mars Bar thrown in to sustain us. Out came the black and gold card, looking as much in place as a donkey in the Grand National. We duly mumbled our thanks before heading off to pick up our clubs.

Having always avoided busy courses by playing at a time of day when others did not, it came as a bit of a surprise that we were in something of a queue on the first tee. Hi-Viz and his friend, still in their jackets, had been followed by two de-motivated looking day-release students, and already we could see a short, large man climbing out of his black cab and heading up to take his place behind us. A couple of girls of college age looked as though they were going to follow him on, but then seemed to think better of it at the last minute.

'Local Rule 1,' said the Undergraduate under his breath as we waited for the students to get clear of the 136 yard first hole. 'You can drop a stroke for each condom you find, 2 strokes if it's been used.'

'How are you supposed to tell?' I asked, but it suddenly didn't seem important.

'And another,' added the Cabinet Maker immediately clutching at it, 'for any dead animal you come across'. The tail of a recently defunct squirrel overflowed enigmatically from a plastic coffee cup that leant against the right hand tee box. The rest of its body was nowhere to be seen.

By now the day-release students had moved off the first green and The Banker settled himself for his shot. Whether we articulated it or not, each of us was lost in our private belief that we would get round this course in a record score and that our game was built for better things than this. Deprived of the scenic beauty of the South Downs as the backdrop, we were persuaded to feel far more confidence than any part of our individual games entitled us to.

At the top of the Banker's inaugural backswing a large man in track suit bottoms and a singlet ran awkwardly across the fairway in front chasing a Staffordshire Bull Terrier, shouting expletives at it as it trotted into a small birch grove to extrude a prolonged crap.

Rule 3, we all agreed, would have to be a one-shot penalty for a ball coming to rest in excrement and having to be moved.

The Banker elegantly fired off his first shot, an un-teed 8 iron if I remember rightly, which veered wildly off to the left, into the grounds of the adjacent hospital and out of bounds. The Cabinet Maker's was no better, fetching up in the middle of what was billed as a bunker, but was in fact a shallow bed of rock hard sand with a thin, oily pool of water in its centre. Only the Undergraduate found the green, and only then, having massively over-hit his tee shot, as the first-bounce staging post on its long outward voyage towards the attractions of Central London on the far distant horizon beyond.

The sounds of Tupac Shakur filtered out of an apartment block window, a fitting soundtrack to what was going on below.

'I don't give a fuck', sang Tupac, as The Cabinet maker toed his third shot into the rhododendrons. Nor did we to be honest.

'They done pushed me to the limit I'm all in', he went on, as the Undergraduate called out from a neighbouring thicket that he had found a dead pigeon and was claiming the extra shot.

'Gotta step lightly cos cops tried to snipe me. The catch. They don't want to stop at the brother man'. It was compelling stuff, almost as compelling as the Banker, in his designer over-trousers, trying to find somewhere to launder his hands after retrieving his third shot from the asbestos-contaminated waters of the bunker.

'How much shit can a N***a take?' We couldn't answer that one, but we could have if he had asked how much shit there was just off the first green, once we had putted out for 5, 6, 7 and 8 respectively. There was a lot and it hadn't by any means all come out of the Staffie. There was waste material in evidence from a wide section of London wildlife: dogs, foxes, Canada geese, and rabbits to name but a few. Any possible mystery about where London's copious wildlife went to relieve itself had been solved before our very eyes.

We might have initially assumed that we were clever and well bred and sophisticated, but that Central London Golf Centre had other ideas. It was designed for better players than us.

Our immediate problem was that the day-release kids had lost their balls in the long grass off the second fairway, so we couldn't progress, and the taxi driver behind was signalling furiously that we should let him play through, so we couldn't relax either. So we just stood on the second tee and waited till it was safe to play, breathing in the South London air and the softening words of Tupac.

'Punk, gay, sensitive little dick bastards'.

He had a point.

*

By the time we got to the fourth tee (413 yards), my game, new clubs or not, was imploding.

It had taken me 22 shots (including 2 lost balls) to get

round the first three holes. Any illusion that I was too good for this course that we had patronisingly selected was crumbling in the asbestos-laden dust of my imagination. 10% of my problem was that the grass on the fairway, if I ever actually found it with a shot, was longer than the rough in many other golf clubs. 90% of it was that I remained what it said 'on the tin', an all-too fragile golfer. As I stood to wait my turn in driving off I watched a cormorant come in to land on a small pond on the edge of an industrial unit. It looked as depressed and hopeless as I felt, and for a second we were brothers in our struggles. It occurred to me that this was the sort of club from which legends were sculpted; ones where the newest star in the golfing firmament has graduated against all odds and made it to the top. This was Rocky 6, but for not very tough people. We had come back into earshot of another rapper by this stage, identified by the Undergraduate as Skepta:

'You need to jump out of the water like Free Willy', he shouted. And he was very possibly right, but all the water here had trolleys in it, which made what he was suggesting a lot more challenging.

The other 3 had all hit decent shots and had adopted a level of quiet smugness that is the sole preserve of a golfer who knows that they are not the worst player out there. I played mine and then watched as the combination of sidespin and wind-force carved it round to the left and into another industrial bunker. The taxi driver, who was a fat and grumpy Glaswegian called Geoff, threw me a lifeline and, in doing so, changed the course of my round.

'Local rule,' he shouted as he went past up the 2nd. 'Ye can move the little fucker back tae the fairway.'

I wasn't entirely sure which little fucker he was referring to, there being 3 human ones in my immediate area, but I took him to mean the ball and duly moved it to an advantageous lie before anyone could correct his instruction, if it happened to be wrong. That little bit of kindness changed the dynamics of my round, and I started to hit the ball in the vague vicinity of where I wanted it to go, a development not lost on the Cabinet Maker. Happily, what he said was drowned out by Mr Skepta:

'That's why they call me a bad boy' (repeat x 8).

We waved Geoff through on the 5th, having added local Rule 4 ('Used surgical gloves on the green may be moved without penalty'), and immediately afterwards, Rule 5 ('Police sirens do not constitute of themselves a man made obstruction, and therefore must be played through') to our growing list. Geoff immediately slowed down to a snail's pace and contrived to lose both balls he was playing in the long grass, presumably fulminating about what the evolution of Uber had done to his business.

Geoff's dramatic loss of speed allowed us a little more time to breathe in our surroundings, and for the Undergraduate to check on Tinder whether there was anyone fit and available living in the vicinity. A couple of teenage girls sat on a bank near where we were, each looking in her own chosen direction, each texting her own invisible thoughts to her own invisible friend somewhere out there in the vastness of SW19.

The 6th tee provided players with a challenging short hole over a pond full of bull rushes, nesting Canada geese and discarded trolleys. As we ate our Mars Bars it began to dawn on us that just about everyone we had met here, with the temporary exception of Geoff, had been both friendly and helpful. The rules were few and the vistas far from idyllic, but it was a little oasis of fun and a genuine challenge for people like us, even if it was set in the midst of the post-industrial landscape around it. Here, under the Heathrow flight path, and hard by bus routes 44 (Tooting Station) and 270 (Mitcham Commonside), lurked the kind of golf we instinctively understood, and which understood us in return.

We looked to the Cabinet Maker for a suitably Marxist commentary on it all, but all he could come up with was a towering hook into a primary school playground alongside.

'Fore!' he mumbled inaudibly, as his Srixon 1 rattled

between the legs of the hop-scotching children of South West London.

'Sorry,' he added even more quietly, as a cheerful boy in glasses and a patka picked it up and added it to his personal collection for resale to the Pro's shop in due course. He waved sympathetically at the Cabinet Maker through the high fence, and the Cabinet Maker grimaced back.

*

Just as some of the great players in golfing history have buried their dreams among the beauty of the azaleas of Augusta, so other lesser mortals have sometimes found their glory among the syringes and turds of municipal courses like this one. But then again, Augusta is a mirage. Allegedly, it is a place where the ambient bird song is mixed in for the microphones by tape; the azaleas are artificially frozen in warm years to stop them flowering before the Masters and blue food dye is mixed into the water to make it look just that little bit more perfect. There was no element of mirage about this London course and none either about my tiny yet spectacular resurgence on its last 3 holes.

We waited for Geoff again on the 7th, once again thrashing around in the undergrowth. He seemed to be making a point, having gone past us, of going as slowly as he possibly could. I was a minimum of 6 strokes worse than anyone in my foursome and had resigned myself to providing the drinks afterwards in order to buy the silence of the other 3 players.

But, when it came to my turn, my tee shot did what it hadn't done all day. It went high, and straight, and the right distance, and ended up about 8 feet from the pin. I held the pose to create the illusion of routine and to give the others a chance to say encouraging things.

'You'll 4 putt from there,' said the Cabinet Maker. Even if he was right, that would turn out to be 4 less than he would eventually take from his current position 5 feet down in the mud of the River Wandle, and 3 less than the Undergraduate would contrive from a pile of wood chippings on the next door fairway.

But I didn't. I went down in par. Then I went and did the same again at the penultimate hole, bringing myself to parity or better with the others. Whereas all I could previously see around me was the cold and rainy landscape of high-rise, urban Britain, now I could see chestnut blossom in the sunshine, seagulls and gleaming red buses. I suddenly felt more at home here than in virtually any other sporting venue I had ever been to.

It was something of a rarity that we all reached the 9th (and last) hole with everything to play for. Normally, one of us (seldom me, it has to be said), had established such a lead by that stage that not even the kind of self-destructive implosions that we all (and a host of professional golfers as well) were capable of could change things. True, the Undergraduate and the Banker had both sustained sufficient damage on the previous two holes to ensure that they would need a miracle to prevail, but I was within one shot of the Cabinet Maker and no bravado on his part was going to strip away the momentum that was going with me.

We arrived on the tee, looked ahead, and saw water.

As a rule, we don't do water well in our little group, finding that the presence of any liquid between where we happen to be and where the pin happens to be has a magnetic effect on our strokes. Back in bucolic Sussex, moorhens stir uneasily in the reeds when they hear us approach and amphibians batten down the hatches for what might follow. So it added a whole heap of extra spice to the final hole to discover that there was a picturesque pond stretching from one side of the fairway to the other, preventing access to the green by anything other than a plucky, lofted shot with added backspin. In theory this favoured the Cabinet Maker, who was actually quite competent at the lofted approach shot, rather than my own brand of scuffed 'chip and run' that relied entirely on their being no bunkers, no bushes and absolutely no water hazards between me and the target. To my certain knowledge, I had never applied backspin to anything, let alone a golf ball. The nearest I had ever got to backspin was watching it on the telly. There was rather less chance of my clearing that pond than there was of the French allowing their entry into the Eurovision Song Contest to be sung in English.

'It's all about balls,' said the Banker. 'Who is going to lay up and pussy across the shortest bit of water, and who is going to actually go for it?'. He was talking the talk of the London financial community; the talk that had brought the world banking system to the brink of disintegration and we would have expected no less from him. This was personal coaching from Gordon Gekko himself.

I hadn't intended to go for it originally. I was content to be a pussy and capitalise on the probable mistakes of others. But something in the Banker's voice demanded a show of something exceptional. That tiny pilot light of ambition that lurks in every physically diminished male of a certain age stuttered into life and glowed for a second or two.

Before the others could bang on about how useless I was, and before they could tell me how they hoped my little Callaway 4 liked swimming, I teed the ball up and hit it without a practice swing. It soared high up in the air, over the pond and out into an area of rough beyond, beside the Crazy Golf course that was adjacent. Rory McIlroy would have kicked himself and broken down in tears to have played such an awful stroke, but for me at that stage it was as close to sporting perfection as I could ever aspire to. I might never find my ball; I might lose the match yet. But I was across the pond and no one could ever take that achievement away from me. Besides, everyone else had yet to do it.

I can't even remember what the other two did with their shots. The key was that the Cabinet Maker planted his in the pond. As he did with the second. As he did with the third. Meltdown, having previously merely tapped him on the shoulder from time to time, now moved into his house with its family and most of their in-laws, and it didn't look as if it was moving out any time soon. This was a ghastly Gothic parody of Jordan Speith falling to pieces at the 12th at the 2016 Masters, and the great news was that I was Danny Willett.

The others gave me exactly 3 minutes to find my ball, or face the consequence of a drop and the resulting penalty. All I could remember about it was that it had come close to peppering Geoff on his way back to the clubhouse, and that he was somewhere near a bunch of Lithuanians working on the Crazy Golf course when it happened. I asked them where it had gone and they hunched their Slavic shoulders in contempt in return. As it was I found it perched encouragingly on a tuft of grass only yards from the edge of the green, and the Cabinet Maker knew that his round was effectively dead.

It was all over bar the gloating. I managed not to mess up

my subsequent chip onto the green and couple of putts and we all duly shook hands under the baleful gaze of Geoff clambering back into his gleaming black cab. In the end I had won, and won comfortably, even if I didn't realise at the time that this was the last time I would win a match outright for four months.

The only thing that remained to be done was a visit to the Tripadvisor site to correct the prevailing impression that this was a rubbish course. It wasn't. It was a magnificent course. As a launching pad for what might be to follow in the rest of the year, condoms, Staffie turds and all, it was nigh on perfect.

*

Towards the end of our round, the Cabinet Maker had gone unusually quiet.

We knew him well and realised that this was not the gritty silence of competition, or even the thoughtful silence of planned revenge. He actually looked dejected. We asked him why.

'I shouldn't read emails when I'm out and about enjoying myself. No good ever comes of it.'

We assumed that something had happened at work and that, instead of regaling us with his record monthly sales figures, as he had become tediously wont to do, some bit of machinery had packed up, or another of his delivery drivers had punctured his radiator by hitting a pheasant at speed.

But, it turned out that a close friend that he had been brought up alongside had died that morning having never really regained consciousness after an operation for Pancreatic Cancer three days before. He was 47 and had 3 children under 10.

'4 weeks, that's all. 4 bloody weeks from tummy ache to ...' He searched for a suitable word, but it didn't come. '... this.'

Then he had looked down at his ball and hit his best shot of the day, high over another pond, and on to the green.

'We're so lucky, you know. Doing this.' He had waved his club around the course, and, by inference, at the fun we were having. 'We can afford it; we can take the day off to do it; we can enjoy the moments of glory, the making tits of ourselves. We can be with friends. Real friends, who don't give a toss how crap we might be. Above all, we're alive, and we're fit enough to enjoy it all. We've just got to go on doing it for ever, because you never know. Do you?'

We didn't know, but we knew he was right. Here, on one of the most basic golf courses in the country, accompanied by some of the lousiest players in the Northern Hemisphere, we were the luckiest people alive. We had all had the normal run of challenges in our lives, but we were blessed to a degree that seemed ruthlessly unfair when we thought of a young father not yet even cold in his bed. The only responsible thing to do was go to a pub and raise a glass to his mate as soon as possible.

'It's on me,' said the Undergraduate, before adding quietly: 'Dad. Can you sub me a twenty.'

Chapter 5

BANKS AND BUNKERS

The art of the outside appointment

'*Eighteen holes of golf will teach you more about your foe than
eighteen years of dealing with him across a desk*'.
Grantland Rice, *US sports columnist, author*

It had all looked rather different in a Chicago restaurant
on a bitterly cold night some two months before.

'I'm coming to Scotland to play a week of golf in May.'
The successful and charismatic leader of a Seattle-based
company that I represented in the UK was reflecting on
my revelation that I had taken up 'proper' golf. 'Why don't
you come and join us for a day or two?'

When he named the courses that he was going to play,
I could think of about a hundred good reasons why not.
These were big, world class, ball-breaking, confidence-
sapping courses that would bleed the very dignity out
of sporting minnows like me. They would set me up on
the first tee and then spit me out among their bunkers,

burns and braes until I was a mere atomic signature of wretchedness on the 18th. Turnberry, Loch Lomond, Troon … the list went on. The people who played these courses had designer shirts and range finders, not to mention woolly club cosies for those misty Caledonian nights. But above all they had talent ability and practise, three notions that I only ever saw from a distance, like ships passing my iceberg in the night.

'I'm a bit tied up that week,' I said. There are very few people in the Northern Hemisphere who consistently get themselves into such deep and regular trouble as I do by volunteering for unsuitable things, but even I knew when to say 'no'.

'Dude, I haven't even told you what week yet!' This was true. He had not. But I had panicked at the mere thought of it.

'May's not a good month, workwise,' I said. 'Besides, you really don't want me spoiling your round by …'

He drained his glass of Tualatin Valley, stared at me in a disappointed way and continued eating.

I thought about it for a while and came to the conclusion that I wanted to leave the conversation slightly less to my disadvantage.

'I'll tell you what, David,' I said. 'If a couple of you come down to Sussex once you've finished in Scotland, we'll let you take us on there.' I named a few minor courses to put him off.

'Sounds unmissable, Dude,' he said, in a way that reflected no disappointment whatsoever. 'Maybe next year.'

Which comment made the arrival of an email three weeks later something of a surprise.

'Arriving London 5 May with my buddy, Jim. All yours till 8th. Get practising, loser.'

*

It is somehow strange that golf has established itself as a currency in the world of building business relationships. An activity that demands total obedience from just about every muscle group in the body, that needs complete concentration and that can reduce an otherwise confident man to a gibbering halfwit in mere minutes, would not appear on the face of it to leave much room for establishing useful commercial progress. After all, you are hardly likely to want to give a giant 5 year construction contract to a man who has just hurled his hybrid club 60 foot up an oak tree.

'Think of it as a six hour sales call,' says Bill Storer, the President of Business Golf Strategies in New Jersey, whilst at the same time persuading us to choose our partners wisely ("play decision makers, not good golfers"); to avoid alcohol and not to discuss business before the 5th hole or after the 15th. Mr Storer has clearly never seen our little foursome, which talks incessantly from the first tee onwards and which finds an alcohol-free round rather daunting, to be honest.

Supporters of golf as a business device argue that people of any age can play it; that the handicap system enables anyone to play anyone else in an interesting game; that the stop-start nature of the game allows for lots of chat in between shots and that it is a fine test of character. Opponents would ask: 'why spoil even further a walk that has been spoiled already?' They might then add that a crime scene of personal humiliation is no place at all to try and do a deal. Personally, at that stage, there was no part of my golf game, or my conduct on a golf course, that I would want anyone to associate with what I might be like to do business with.

Having said that, the same day as my friend's email arrived the Economist published some research that said that bosses who played golf were paid, on average, 17% more than those who did not. So I emailed the Cabinet Maker and the Banker:

'American supplier and his mate coming to play golf with us on May 6 and 7, having failed to understand that we

can't play. Apparently plays off nothing, and regularly beats Phil Mickelson. You need to masquerade as grown-ups for an afternoon each, and support the cause. If you do this, I will buy you supper. If you don't, I will never speak to you again. Or at least not until either of you become properly rich yourself.

PS Apparently you'll earn more if you do this'

The Banker, who was probably staring into a screen saver full of rotating pound signs and wondering what his next company car might be when the email arrived, came straight back.

'Delighted to support you. Where and when?

PS Does your friend need any asset financing?

PPS Just asking'.

I assured him that my American colleague was really only visiting the UK in order to find the best rates for asset financing, and had specifically asked me if I knew any people who were involved in providing it.

The Cabinet Maker was harder to read:

'Get fucked.'

I pointed out that the Banker would therefore have to play twice then, get two suppers, and probably become obscenely rich through the contacts he made on the day. Besides, it was well known in our industry that the American was only over in the UK looking for someone to make him cabinets. He only had to look in the trade press and he would see it for himself.

'OK. Only if I don't have to play with you. Send details.'

In military terms, I was already on the Start Line and ready for battle.

*

Over the next few weeks, our golf took on a distinctly urgent, more intense, feel. Two mornings a week we would meet at first light at a local 9 hole course and race around in time to change into work clothes and be in our respective workplaces before 9 o'clock. When shots were fluffed, we would give each other well-intentioned advice rather than naked abuse. When our opponent performed some majestically competent effort, we would quietly celebrate, where previously we would have poured scorn over it. For the first time we were working more as a team and less as a band of warring factions from some Mongolian military subculture. At the weekend we would put in a full 18 holes and then pick the pieces out of it afterwards with the help of a 20 year old David Leadbetter self-help book that my mother-in-law had given me in the years when there was still some hope that parts of me could be improved.

The imminent arrival of the Americans, one with a handicap of 7 and the other 9, had allowed a little bit of steel to enter into our collective soul. It was not just our individual games at stake, it was the whole reputation of the Mother Country we were fighting to uphold. In the vacuums that passed for our mid-life brains I think we really may have started to believe that we could bridge the gap between comparative incompetence and their rare mastery in the space of a few early morning practice sessions. If only the oxygen-wasting Dementor down in North Cornwall could see us now!

Late one evening, another email arrived, this time from the Banker.

'Watch attached Youtube clip on how to create a lag in golf swing. The guy's a git, but he seems to get some real snap in his wrists, and club head speed.'

I duly watched it and then took a club up into the pitch black garden and gave it a go. It was half past eleven on a Saturday evening and I was a Lagavullin to the good. It all seemed to work but then, after a Lagavullin, everything seems to work. I absent-mindedly sent a ball careering over the neighbouring park wall and imagined its lonely passage eastwards over the adjoining deer park and on into the night. I repeated the action a couple of times and then went back in to recharge the glass and check the emails.

'Just seen this one on squaring your clubface. Makes sense, but I really don't like that green shirt he's wearing. What do you think?'

I went back onto the lawn with the glass and a few more balls. The swing appeared better than ever. Five minutes later I went back in.

'There's a cracker here on improving your club path. Attached. Gotta try this next time out.'

And on it went. On the screen, it all seemed so easy. In the car on the way to the course, it all seemed so easy. In the changing room, it all seemed so easy. On the driving range, it all seemed so easy. So what in God's name happened between practise and reality; in those final steps up onto the first tee when it started to count?

*

David's friend was called Jim and he was waiting in the car park when I called at the hotel to collect them for the first of our two games. He was standing by a bag of clubs that, had it been able to show emotion, would have been crying with laughter at me and my own set. Our sense of mythology required Jim to be a senior executive at Microsoft and to be brash, humourless and uncompromising on the golf course. Instead, he turned out to run a collection of restaurants in Seattle and was, from the start, self-effacing, gentle and funny.

'How was Scotland?' I asked, filling in the minutes whilst David completed the process of looking 20 years younger than he actually was upstairs in the hotel.

'Cold and wet, actually' said Jim, as if being cold and wet in Scotland was some extraordinary freak of natural history. 'But the golf was great and so were the evenings up at Loch Lomond. Just happy to be here in the sunshine.' It was hard to argue with him on this score. England looks perfect on only about 2 days each year and, by timing his visit to this weekend, he had hit the jackpot.

Up at the club we paired David with the Cabinet Maker, meaning that Jim drew the short straw with me. Until now, I think we all had a notion that this was going to be a question of USA vs UK, but we realised the idiocy of this before a solitary club had been extracted from a bag.

'Four ball, better ball?' I suggested.

David looked at my bag of proud new irons with disappointment bordering on incomprehension.

'You playing with them?' he asked, as if the Equipment Fairy would suddenly bound out of the shrubbery with a bag of Taylor Made M1s and deposit them in my lap.

There we stood, the four of us, on the first tee; the last time for four hours that David and Jim would genuinely not know what they were up against. As far as they were concerned we might be modest and understated Brits; gritty and determined stealth fighters underneath a veneer of deadly Edwardian charm and super cheap kit. They were probably wary of the quality ambush that they thought we might be about to spring. But the Cabinet Maker's first shot disabused them of any such notions as it soared in an increasingly violent rightwards arc, towards a group of ladies coming up the 18th fairway, and came to rest against a tree shelter.

David took an unfeasibly vast driver out of his bag and swung it murderously hard a couple of times before addressing the ball. There was something rather awesome about the practise shots themselves, let alone the drive that followed, as the base of the club head kissed the turf below it at around 110 mph. The difference between the Cabinet Maker's first shot and David's practise swing was a sufficient predictor of what would follow as to encourage lesser men to abandon the game at that point. He took his stroke and watched it fly 240 yards towards the hole.

'Shame,' said Jim quietly. 'You were nailing those earlier in the week.'

When it was our turn, much the same thing happened, only my ball slewed off into a shelter belt of oak trees to the left and Jim's went about 10 yards beyond David's.

Other than on the telly, we had never seen golf balls travel so far.

'Dude. I guess you must have rolled your wrists on that one. Pity.' And it became clear to us at that early moment that David and Jim were relentlessly competitive and mocking with each other, just like the Cabinet Maker and me, only on an altogether different plane of excellence. Somehow it seemed more elegant the way they did it.

When we had retrieved my ball and got to Jim's, he took out a range finder and fixed it on the pin. The introduction of technology suddenly made me feel grown up; like the first time I bought a girl a drink. I wanted my local friends to see me standing there with a real golfer, discussing a challenging shot through the medium of a $750 bit of kit. They would think that I had finally arrived.

'That's about 170 yards from here,' he said. Looks like you need a long 6 iron or a short 5.' He reflected for a bit, unaware that I could still only dream of the kind of yardages that were meat and drink to him. 'Just take your time.'

'Only one rule in my golf,' he added as I pulled the new 6 iron out of my bag. 'No one ever says "sorry".' Apologising for what I had just done was a major part of my sporting armoury, so what he was demanding of me put me under more pressure than he could have possibly imagined.

In the context of my ability, what followed was little short of miraculous. I didn't scuff it 50 yards along the fairway, and I didn't heave it off over the steep wooded bank to my left. Instead, I hit it hard, straight and low towards the flag and watched it bounce a couple of times before making its merry way onto the green. It didn't matter that the shot represented an unrepeatable sequence of unplanned biometric miracles, or that it had no right to be where it was. It was factual history and it could not be rewound.

'See?' said Jim. 'Nothing whatsoever wrong with that.'

Much the same was happening with the others. We only realised much later on when we discussed it together after they had returned to the USA, that David and Jim had simply removed all the haste and rush from our games, and consequently allowed us to be as good as we could be, as opposed to as bad as we feared we were doomed to be.

We each putted out and headed off towards the rest of the round, with the Cabinet Maker idly wondering at what stage he could bring up the subject of the potential market for cabinets in Washington State.

*

The next few holes brought out the best golf I had ever played up to that point, and they did the same for the Cabinet Maker. Deprived of undue speed and with the benefit of quietly offered advice, we both reached a state of sporting grace normally reserved for those who had been more blessed by the Co-ordination Fairy. For a brief moment in time, all the scuffs, shanks, hooks, toe hits and pushes that punctuated our usual rounds had packed their bags and temporarily disappeared. We knew that they would be back, and soon, but we rejoiced in their temporary absence. Knowing that these people had travelled 4000 miles to come and play with us instilled a rare and respectful discipline into the way we played, and it made a difference. We, who had only glimpsed excellence through a glass darkly, could rejoice for an instant at meeting it face to face. To be fair, both we and 'it' knew that the association was unlikely to be a long one. That's the thing about excellence: it chooses its friends carefully.

On the 3rd hole, Jim put his drive within 18 inches of the hole, so I didn't have to play at all. On the 4th, we put ourselves 2 up courtesy of the Cabinet Maker's enthusiastic 3rd shot piling over the back of the green. On the 5th, embracing the demons of ambition, I even outdrove Jim and had the luxury of watching him play the next shot, mine being the better placed of the two. On the 6th, we watched David bend his shot deliberately round the canopy of a huge oak tree, and put the ball on a green that had been all but invisible when he was lining up. On the 530 yard 8th, Jim and I were on the fringe of the green in 2 shots, gently fist-pumping our delight while David was having to sort out his partner's error of judgement behind a fallen tree. On the 9th, I found the green with my drive for the first time ever. For a brief moment in time I was joining the Corinthians, and it felt decidedly good.

Playing with Jim was like walking into school arm in arm with the class bully: the others might hate you but, when the Big Boy's around, they can't do anything about it. I took a photo of the front 9 scorecard (exactly 40) and sent it off to the Undergraduate by way of a parental 2 fingered salute. After all, he must need rousing from his exam revision from time to time. The texted reply was terse:

'That's his. Where's yours?'

Whilst ungracious, he did have a point.

*

Things didn't start unravelling until the 12th, by which time we were firm friends and it really didn't matter.

My attention span had been tested to its limits in the previous couple of hours and I had decided to blast the next ball to Kingdom Come which, in the event, turned out to be a small spot of heather about 5 yards to the left of the Lady's Tee.

Skill, for sportsmen like me, is like a rare visiting bird that winter brings fleetingly into the garden. When it first arrives amongst the bird feeders, it is a beautiful and welcome guest, and its presence lifts the heart. For a time you think that it might stay for ever, that its natural space is your little patch of ground, but then it flies home, or the neighbours' cat kills it, and you are back to square one. The other three were silent as I walked the few paces required to retrieve my ball.

At this point, I needed the symmetry of the Cabinet Maker producing a similar shot to make me feel less exposed, but he didn't oblige. He, David and Jim all drove their balls firmly and pointedly straight down the middle, and all three headed off together whilst I went to retrieve my ball. I texted him:

'I suppose that makes you a golfer, then?'

To add insult to injury, his turned out to have been was the better drive and so David was playing the second shot. It gave him time to text back:

'Quiet. It's 3 against 1 now. You might as well go home'.

A few seconds later, a further text appeared:

'He's buying a work surface. That's how good I am.'

*

Implosion or not, Jim and I won the round with relative ease and, if anything, the sun was beating down with even more enthusiasm the following afternoon. We kept the same pairings, substituting the in-form Banker for the erratic Cabinet Maker, and the round unfolded in much the same way. In a first for me, I was playing two days running and with a measure of confidence. The Banker was doubly excited. First, that he was playing against grown-up business people from across the pond and, secondly, because he had learned that David had just successfully sold his company and become the kind of person that the Banker wanted eventually to be. The proximity to financial success, something our regular foursome denied him, always made him excited, and he celebrated by purchasing yet another garment from the Pro's shop.

David, who had only slept a few hours in the previous couple of nights what with the general roistering up at Loch Lomond, had been out of sorts on the first day, but suddenly announced himself with a couple of 8 foot putts around the turn, followed by some all-round excellent play. It provided a tiresome dilemma for me, to the effect that whilst I am a competitive soul who wants quite badly to win, he was an important supplier who I wanted quite badly to have a nice and ultimately successful day. But once again the dice fell for Jim and I, or rather for Jim and the occasional short putt from me.

We finished in a quintessentially English pub, performing the quintessentially English trick of trying to fix up the next visit before the current one had even come to an end. We traded pints at the same velocity as we swapped stories of the round; of what might have been, and what probably never was and, as we traded them, we began to see through the alcoholic haze the tiresome requirement to surrender yet another prejudice. If this was 'business' golf, we said, then bring it on, bring it on.

Wiser men might just have left it there.

*

The very next day, and in a fit of hubris that wouldn't have disgraced Socrates, if hubris is what Socrates did, I emailed the Buying Director of one of my largest customers. He was due to come down to visit our office the following week and was staying over once we had done our work. He had a reputation of being an outstandingly good player and I was quietly determined to see how far we could push this thing.

'Do you fancy a quick round of golf when you come down next week? If so, bring clubs.' I knew he played off an obscenely low handicap and that he liked to do things well. I also knew that my company relied to some considerable extent on his goodwill, which made the decision a strange one to say the least.

'Sure. Never knew you played.' Was that enthusiasm, forbearance, or the sound of a man humouring a small child?

'I have my moments.'

The truth was that, up until recently, I could count my 'moments' on the fingers of one finger, to a shot that dated back to another decade, and might not even have been played by me now I come to think about it.

'Glad to hear that. Looking forward to it'.

He might have been but, now that he had said 'yes', I certainly wasn't. And neither would he be once he was up to his neck in pine needles helping to look for his supplier's ball. I emailed the Cabinet Maker.

'Major buyer of mine coming down; looking for new stuff, particularly in the work surface line. 18 holes should be long enough to explain it all. 4.00 pm next Thursday'.

And then the Banker.

'Networking opportunity for you on Thursday at 4. Do you do stock financing?'

Once I had picked up the really bad words out of the Cabinet Maker's reply, and harvested the pathetic willingness from the Banker's, I had a four-ball, which was all that counted.

What we weren't to know was that the larger part of our

small group would be struck by a devastating piece of deceit between now and the game.

*

It arrived 2 days before the Buying Director's visit in the form of another email from the Cabinet Maker, entitled 'Eat my dust', and was a scanned copy of his brand new handicap certificate, awarded after his appearance at his club's 9 hole pitch and putt 'roll-up' event the evening before. His name was there in red, in between a deputy head teacher and a monosyllabic local printer. It said '25'.

His relationship with this club had always been akin to one of cheating husband and mistress, minus the sex and expensive jewellery, or possibly including it. Over the last few weeks he had wasted no moment, we now discovered, to go and get in a few holes while no one was looking. Heading off to work, back from work, walking the dogs or even in between meetings, he would slide off down there to improve his swing. He had become a regular golf club saddo, alternating between filling his days with it and then pretending to the rest of us that he didn't give a damn. His diary, which had previously incorporated a fine mix of Toms, Davids and Rogers, was suddenly full to the brim with Grahams, further Grahams and then yet more of them. He could have got a cut price ride to virtually any airport in Britain, so long as he paid cash.

But, in acquiring that handicap, he had broken one of the

cardinal rules of our gang. He had dared to short circuit the laborious and stuttering process of moving onwards, and had then compounded the sin by crowing about it. The way the rest of us looked at it was this: if the best he could achieve on a course that more than likely boasted a couple of yellow bridges and a hole in a clown's mouth was 25, then he had a lifetime of disappointment ahead of him.

*

Our business done, the Buying Director and I headed up to the course to meet the others. He looked me up and down as we emerged from the changing room in my increasingly classy kit.

'I thought we were playing golf, not moving furniture,' he said.

I ignored him and pulled my new £40 Callaway-Lite bag out of the car boot with a proud flourish, and watched the legs flick out suggestively as its base touched the tarmac. I gave him an, 'I'll see your five and raise you ten' look, that might have been better placed had his collection not been quite so superior to my American Golf promotional stuff. It seemed like the soundtrack of my career in this benighted sport was forever doomed to be the noise of sharp intakes of breath punctuated with occasional mocking laughter.

'Is that what you're playing with?' He looked genuinely concerned that I must have grabbed the wrong bag when leaving home and picked up an 8 year old child's set instead of mine.

This threw up a problem that is presumably common to those who mix business with sport, viz that, through the inadvisability of telling your important customer where, and how far, to stick it, you inevitably end up in silence and with rising blood pressure.

The Cabinet Maker had done his research and was dribbling at the prospect of 4 hours partnering a man with a buying budget of close to £100 million, and not a seamless work surface yet to be seen in his collection. Embarrassingly so, in fact. It was also not lost on him that two players had handicaps and two didn't. Up on the first tee he introduced himself to the Buying Director.

'I play off 25,' he announced casually, as if anyone cared; as if anyone was even listening. The air was alive with the sound of the local wildlife boring itself to sleep; of yawning squirrels plummeting from the surrounding trees. Playing with the Cabinet Maker was beginning to feel strangely similar to listening to the Wednesday afternoon repeat of *Money Box Live*.

The Banker had also done *his* research, and had established that this was a main board director and therefore someone who had legal and financial responsibilities and probably rarely had the opportunity to meet a fresh face from the world of high finance, let alone a face as shamelessly and boyishly persuasive as his own. He suggested that he should partner the Buying Director.

'Nah. I'll go with him. He looks like he needs my help,' he said, looking in my general direction.

Which nod to the Goldilocks Syndrome turned out to be just as well because, for the first 4 or 5 holes at least, it meant that an 'Excellent' and a 'Dismal' were pitted against two 'OK's' and an equilibrium was established. If the Buying Director's first drive was a bit of a disappointment, the next 17 were anything but. Good golfers have an annoying habit of being able to put the ball more or less where they want it to be put, even if that is a spot 260 yards away, and even when it has had to fly over a 1000 year old oak tree to get there.

A complication was added by the arrival of the Undergraduate and a tall, hairy friend immediately behind us, and of a four-ball of impatient trolley-pushing men of a certain age behind them. They were a visiting foursome from a superior Surrey club. When the topography of the course arranged itself so that we were temporarily right alongside the latter for a minute or two, a sour faced member of the elderly foursome called over.

'You should let that pair behind you through, you know,' he said, presumably concerned that he personally would be held up in a few holes time if we didn't. We weren't holding anyone up and we weren't about to be either.

'We will if we need to, thank you,' said the Buying Director. I dearly wanted to add that if Sour Face knew who the pair in between was, he might have different ideas, but I kept my peace.

'No. That's normal etiquette on a short par 3. You should let them through.' He had the air of a man about to vent his spleen on a junior check-in girl at an airport, simply because she couldn't answer back.

'We're not holding them up and there are people in front of us, but thank you for your advice. We'll let them through if we need to.' The Buying Director wasn't budging, and he had three long decades of experience on better courses than this to back up his point of view.

'Well, I think you should. It's what we do here,' came the reply from the Kindergarten, before he ploughed his approach shot into a huge rhododendron.

Long before the Buying Director's view was justified by finishing the round, and the Undergraduate finishing his, a full half hour in front of Sour-Face, this was the incident that brought us all together, that removed any last vestiges of formality from our round. From then on our guest submitted himself to the cheerful abuse and occasional resentful praise that was part and parcel of how we did it, and why we were slowly starting to fall in love this game. He was very, very good, and we were very, very bad, but the difference mattered not the least to any of us.

Golf for us was an adventure, a return to childhood. It was our *yin* to the *yang* of every day life, our glimpse of the heavens in an otherwise overcast world. It was fellowship and occasional joy. Until this point we had never seen anyone get cross on a course, nor ever got remotely cross ourselves. We weren't any good, but we were respectful of the course and the other people playing on it. However, golf for Sour-Face was merely an extension of the disciplines and hierarchies of the workplace, a metaphor for his endless struggle to amount to be something more than a lone tit moaning in the wilderness.

*

When the game was over we went to the club-house for a drink, to mull over the view, the sunshine and, for the Buyer and me, the satisfactory result. The playing partner from Monday, who had signed off the Cabinet Maker's handicap certificate at the other course, was enjoying a pint on the terrace and took the opportunity of our arrival to wave cordially at his new friend.

'How did you get on?' he said, trying to gauge the reading on the smug-o-meter.

'Good, thanks. I think I played to my handicap … more or less'.

'Oh that!' said his friend. 'I wouldn't worry about that. That's just a local thing for the school course. You can't use it anywhere else.'

There followed a comfortable awkwardness, as when the C List celebrity that no one has heard of turns up to declare the new local garden centre open, and then has to explain to the assembled people who the hell he is.

The colour drained from the Cabinet Maker's face. He had broken the unwritten rule to no effect whatsoever. All the chicanery, the secret rounds, the Monday roll-up, they counted for nothing. It was like buying a Greek Government bond for your child, and then discovering that someone else was the father.

The Banker and I had died and gone to heaven.

Chapter 6

LEADED LIGHTS ALONG
THE DEVIL'S HIGHWAY

Never having to say Surrey

*The trees taunt you; the sand mocks you;
the water calls your name and they say golf is a quiet game.*

Anon

If the Cabinet Maker hadn't turned up late, angry, fresh from a site visit in jeans and covered in plaster, we probably would have got away with it.

An emailed round-robin invitation to "A foursome, normally worth £280, at one of Surrey's most prestigious golf courses" had flopped on to my desk a few weeks before, via a colleague who rated golf somewhere around Dante's sixth circle of hell. 'More your kind of thing than mine,' he had added helpfully at the top. And he was right.

One of the developing pleasures of golf was the notion that you could pick up your kit, your game and your friends, and transplant them to a whole host of different places;

brand new scenery where the folds and nuances of each hole started off a well-kept secret. This not only kept the whole experience fresh, but it added a sense of adventure as well, not least in the concern each time we turned up at a new club that we might somehow be 'found out'. One of the reasons that we all wanted handicaps was that, without them, many of the best courses in the country wouldn't let us on. This one was different: they wanted us on because they wanted to sell us something.

When making the booking it became clear that the expectation behind the invite was that the foursome would consist of captains of industry, each one aching to set up a conference, or something called an 'offsite board meeting', and that we would be required to give half an hour of our time to be shown round by the Business Development Manager as our 'payment' for the round. I emailed the trio accordingly:

'£280 of golf for nothing. Tee off 2.04 on Wednesday 11th. Course quite grown up, so proper kit. If you want to play, you turn up at 1.00 and look interested in what the nice man is going to say to us. I will do the talking.'

The Student was doing an internship in commerce and alcohol abuse in Sydney and was replaced by the Tree Hugger; an old friend who ran a one-man band hedge planting business outside Winchester. That was easy: we would refer to him as a Hedge Fund Manager without even telling an untruth. The Banker could be relied upon to look affluent and clubbable any time, any place, so it was only the Cabinet Maker who gave us cause for concern. The problem with the Cabinet Maker, we had discovered over the years, was that you never knew which one out of Ken Dodd or Karl Marx was going to turn up. It didn't matter too much today as he was running fashionably late, as a series of texts announced.

'M3 full of cones and twats who can't drive. Can you get me a sandwich'.

'Say "please"'.

'Just get me a sodding sandwich'. Only Spellcheck had written down 'sobbing', which seemed, on reflection, apposite.

The Business Development Manager had an air of someone who would rather be anywhere, and doing anything, other than being here and looking after us. Unusually for a tour of conference facilities he started off in the toilets, announcing proudly that they were cleaned once an hour, as if this had somehow presented us with the secret of alchemy. Next up was the Surrey Suite and Boardroom, which he told us had complimentary wireless internet connection, SMART Board and the necessary supporting equipment for 160 delegates, sitting 'theatre style'. Guiltily we stared down at our feet, knowing that we didn't even know 160 suitable people between us, let alone ones who could morph into grown-up delegates at a grown-up Golf Club.

The Tree Hugger, whose career in amateur dramatics spanned 3 decades, decided it was time to make a contribution.

'How far in advance would my company need to book the Boardroom?' he asked. Given that his company consisted of him plus a bloke called George who helped out in the deep midwinter with the planting, we were impressed by his cheek. The only part of this that was problematical was that he looked less like a hedge fund manager than anyone in Europe; the Northern Hemisphere perhaps. There were animals burrowing under my garden shed that made more convincing hedge fund managers than him. He had the wild hair, un-ironed shirt and ruddy middle-aged complexion of a man who spent most of his life outdoors and the demeanour of one for whom asset mix, hurdle rate and risk arbitrage were hieroglyphics from a distant civilisation. When the Tree Hugger employed leverage, it was normally with a large shovel in the rich Hampshire loam.

'I'll email you our online booking system,' said the Manager, eyeing him with the infinite sadness of a man whose life has simply gone in the wrong direction and who knew instinctively that the Tree Hugger's Board meetings could in all probability take place on the driver's seat of his Mitsubishi Pick-up. Which, being a sole trader, they could. In fact, for many years, I happen to know that his AGM took place in the choir stalls of Winchester Cathedral as he sat completing his paperwork in the seat he had reserved for the popular carol concert that was to follow 2 hours later.

Meanwhile, the Banker, wholly in his element in this kind of venue, was probing the benefits of the Loyalty Swipe Card and insurance cover for Hole-in-One celebrations and looking every inch like a man who intended to fill the place on semi-regular intervals with people in an alluring array of Pringle sweaters from deep within the Asset Finance world. He was coming over, as he always managed to, as a man who would be boarding a helicopter for Monaco were it not for the tiresome business of having to decide when to trigger Article 50 of the EU Treaty, or proof read the Queen's birthday honours list for any omissions that caught his eye. Five more minutes of this, I was thinking, and we will have done enough to get out onto the course and have our game.

Nothing in this place came from a world I knew. I looked at a little leaflet on the boardroom table, foreshadowing the menus available at the festive season, and each line I read killed a little bit more of my acting ability. There is something about the word 'carvery' that makes a man want to go out and commit headline-grabbing crimes. But, when it is followed by steaks that are 'chaperoned by onion rings and fried tomato wedges', the writing is truly on the wall. The word 'coffee', which would have been perfectly sufficient, had been translated into 'steamy coffee from the lush plantations of Costa Rica'. Ditto tea (Sri Lanka). Ditto chocolate (Brazil). The word 'trimmings', especially when preceded by 'with all the' is a signal from God that it is time to die, or at least get out of the building as soon as decency permits. This, it seemed to me, was a sign of the yawning chasm waiting to engulf us if we ever took the corporate side of this game too seriously.

However, into the middle of it all arrived the Cabinet Maker fresh – in order – from his site visit, the M3, and the toilet. As he was wearing jeans and was covered in a thin film of dust, the Manager not unreasonably thought that he was part of the Club's maintenance staff, and assured him that we would be out of his way in a couple of minutes, after which he could get on with whatever worthy manual labour needed his attention. It probably didn't help that the 3 of us made no effort to recognise or greet him, or that the Manager followed up with a, 'you still here?' look, once it was clear that he had not left the room.

Not to anyone's surprise, up popped Karl Marx.

'I think you'll find I'm here to play golf,' he announced. The Cabinet Maker has an old habit of saying 'I think you'll find'. It is a traditional waymark on his road from sweetness and light to unalloyed grumpiness, so the remaining 3 of us hurriedly made conciliatory noises to both he and the Manager. Effortlessly brushing down the entire British class system into a neat pile of clichés on the Boardroom floor, we made our way to the Pro's shop, and the 18 holes of adventure that lay beyond.

The underlying problem was the fact that we were really starting to get into this game, and that the Manager, although he was only doing his job, was holding us up. Over the course of the Spring and early Summer we had emerged at different speeds out of our primordial soup of incompetence and were now actively caught up in the notion that we really could get better. Possibly much better. Gone were the heirloom canvas bags, the rugby shirts and trainers and, in their place, were the fruits of innumerable trips to American Golf or, in the case of the Banker, the Wentworth Pro's shop. Rather worryingly, we had even started to look like golfers. Whilst we stopped short of the patterned sweaters and the Galvin Green Nash golf trousers, we no longer felt like utter frauds every time we stepped on to the first tee. Slowly, the occasional good shot became the occasional good hole, and then the occasional goodish round. We knew instinctively that, although we might like to think of ourselves as rebels, we were in fact becoming the same as every other Saturday morning golf hero, piling his or her clubs into the car and living the stereotype.

He might have just let us go, but the Manager had the last laugh.

'I need some fresh air,' he said, 'so I'll pop down to the first tee and see you on your way'. Translated into English, every golfer knows that this means: 'I'm pretty sure that I've been sold a pup here with you lot and I'm going to check you out before letting you wreck my course.'

There is a world of difference between you standing on the first tee with 3 friends, idly wondering which of your multiple split personalities will be in attendance today, and you standing on the first tee under the critical gaze of a figure of authority. The latter is like trying to drive sensibly in front of a Police patrol car during the hours of darkness after a single pint, or acting like a grown up the first time you attend a parent's evening as a parent. For a reason that will be familiar to sports psychologists the world over, but is a mystery to me, each of the muscle groups involved in the swing can suddenly develop its own individual, and contrary, take on what is required. The resulting geographical relationship between club head and ball is a vague one, less old friends than ships passing in the night.

We had decided on a four-ball-better-ball formula[12], on the basis that it got us round slightly quicker, and shared out

---

[12] A format whereby a very bad golfer may shelter behind a rather better golfer by playing alternate strokes, and thereby sharing the result.

the misery of underperformance. Up stepped the freshly clad Cabinet Maker and unfurled an annoyingly straight, mid-distance 3 wood, and promptly pretended to lose it in the distance. He held the pose momentarily, as if anyone cared.

However, something other than the ordinariness of the golf seemed now to be diverting the attention of our new friend, the Manager. He was staring down at the bag from which the Tree Hugger was extracting a club, and what he saw there didn't appear to be making him happy. Because what he saw, in stark contrast to the Banker's, whose beautiful hand-crafted irons nestled comfortably within a voluminous bag of hand-stitched leather simply oozing excellence, was a thin and faded beige canvas bag with holes in it, with an even thinner set of wooden sticks poking out of it, and a series of very faded labels attached to it. Whilst the rest of us chose between a Driver and a 3 Wood for the 420 yard first, the Tree Hugger was carefully weighing up between his antique, hickory Diamondback Mid Iron, and the Auchterlonie Special Spoon. Everything in his bag pre-dated World War 2, had known food rationing and was still mesmerised by the idea of colour television. There were clubs in there that had come back from the Indian sub-continent when the Empire fell in 1947 and for whom graphite and carbon fibre were still weak conceptual pulses flickering into earth from outer space. Everything now depended on an exhibition of consummate confidence, at which point the age of the equipment could be set against the skill of its owner, and all would be OK.

It was not to be. Having not played the game for a few months, he had toned down his ambition and initially decided to push the ball down the fairway with the help of his Wooden Cleek. 'Sensible man,' the rest of us thought, believing that he would then deploy the old shoulder injury excuse to explain why it hadn't gone very far. Instead, he suddenly changed his mind and decided to go for glory. He gave the Cleek a homicidal swing, watched the club-head impart the most gentle of kisses to the ball on its way through, and then saw the resulting spin take the ball violently to the right and then arc backwards towards the clubhouse.

'We'll play mine,' said the Cabinet Maker, and the Business Manager turned on his heel to return to his office and check out the 'situations vacant' section of *Golf Monthly*.

*

The summer sunshine beat down on us as we made our way round the front nine, creating conditions in which any course on earth would look good. This particular one had the misfortune to be a *quite good* course in the immediate vicinity of some of the most famous in England, like an Audi dealership sandwiched between Ferrari and Maserati concessions. On the outskirts of Accrington, it might have shone, but hard by the smug leaded lights and satin soft furnishings of Surrey's A30 Belt, it just looked a little aggrieved.

There was a traffic jam building up on the 10th tee due, as far as we could make out, to an unfeasibly huge lady having to be shoe-horned in or out of her buggy. We took the opportunity to sit on the bank, break out the Mars Bars and observe proceedings.

'We've come a long way since last October, you know,' said the Banker, recklessly determined to tempt fate. The Banker was one of life's positive people, always seeking to identify the good in what was going on. We put it down to the size and frequency of his bonus cheques.

We watched the lady in question set the ball down within the arc of her own gravitational pull, and run through some laboured and irregular practise swings.

'But what's the end point? What are we trying to get out of it?'

The Cabinet Maker told him not to complicate things. We settled to watch the large lady execute a violent slice into the reed bed just beyond, and to the right of, the tee. It was a hot day and the enforced break was not unwelcome.

'He's right, though,' I pointed out. 'Our original aim was

to be less than useless. We can all get somewhere near 100 these days. Even me. We'd all get a handicap somewhere or other. We could just about play in a competition, providing it wasn't a very good one. I think we need to expand the repertoire. Create a finale'.

'Meaning?' asked the Cabinet Maker, as the lady re-set a new ball on the tee.

''Meaning,' said the Banker, 'that we need to convince one of the best courses in the country that it wants our custom and play there. And then go back to that Cornish course that wouldn't let Roger play and brandish our handicap certificates.'

'And that's where the adventure can end,' I added quietly.

There was silence as the three other ladies from the four in front demonstrated varying degrees of awfulness.

'But you're going to keep it up, aren't you?' asked the Tree Hugger. 'I mean, all this effort and stuff. You can't just stop.'

The Banker and the Cabinet Maker agreed, but I wasn't so sure.

'No. I think that'll be me, once we've done Cornwall. What I signed up for was a year or so. See where it all led us to. Adventures. That kind of stuff. And then pack it in, like we did with the canoeing, the half marathons, all the other stuff. Try the next thing.'

If I had anything to do with it, I would be like the Skywalker Gibbon, who had taken until 2016 to be identified as a brand new species, only to be announced simultaneously to be on the verge of extinction.

Deep down, I suppose, I harboured a fear that when the novelty wore off, what would be left for me would be a degraded version of the precious thing that we had now. Where there was once novelty, there would be sameness, and where there was adventure, there would be routine. The beauty of the time we were sharing now was that it was all new and, for a reason none of us understood until a little later, very slightly mischievous. Allied to that was the sense that we were being allowed, encouraged even, to do this by people that we loved, who just derived pleasure from seeing us having fun. None of us wanted to become the kind of man who slopes off to the golf course as an act of deception.

'Are you serious?' demanded the Banker. This is the most fun we've ever had together. We could get better. Go travelling all over the place, and enter competitions. I want to grow old doing this now that I've learned it.'

'Yup. We'd go travelling all over the place and become golf

bores. It would become all we talked about. Wouldn't we just become miserable if it started to go wrong, and impossible if we became any good? And then one day we would wake up and we would have been transmogrified into sad old men at the monthly medal, pushing expensive trolleys into the morning mist, whining about foreigners and the soft prison system. Besides, we would need to buy Volvos.'

The Cabinet Maker reflected on this for a while, and then announced that this was precisely the kind of old man he wished to become. 'Anyway, what the hell does 'transmogrify mean?' he asked. 'I thought that was something you did to cats.'

The fourball in front was heaving itself into its tiny looking buggies and it was nearly time for us to carry on.

However, the first divide of our adventure had started to open up. With the marathon running, it was always going to be a matter of time and general creakiness before we gave it up. But, with golf, we could go on until we had at least one foot in the grave. After all, my godfather was still easing his way around the West Sussex at 87, his age and his score remarkably similar. The Banker and the Cabinet Maker were made of similar stuff and had started to understand that they had finally alighted on something they could cheerfully do for the rest of their lives. But I knew myself too well, and what I knew at that moment was that I could never serve that lifelong apprenticeship and still enjoy it. I needed to get to a certain standard and then move on. Out beyond the metaphorical streetlights, there was a world of things that I hadn't even tried yet.

*

The long afternoon wore on, and it was a while before we realised that something strange was going on.

Or not going on. For what we had realised in the last 7 or 8 holes was that we had finally grown up into anonymous golfers, quietly going about our business of getting round eighteen holes without causing distress or chaos. There were a few routinely awful shots, mainly from me, to be sure, and a few expletives, mainly from the Cabinet Maker, but for the first time we could have been just anyone else out on a Wednesday afternoon in high summer. By a process of repetition we had picked up enough good habits over the last year to effectively matriculate into precisely the people we had merely giggled at a year before. Instead of rushing each shot as if that could somehow minimise the visibility, and hence the embarrassment, we were taking our time. Instead of behaving like naughty schoolboys, as if that could somehow show that we weren't taking it seriously, we had started minding. If Phase 1 was those afternoons on the driving range the previous Autumn, and Phase 2 were the early forays onto proper courses, we were now beginning Phase 3. It was a time for celebration, tinged with a tiny regret for the innocence of lost youth.

Things came to a head at the 17th, where a deep and vertically banked stream snaked its way across the fairway at around 160 yards and 2 copses simultaneously came together to complete the pinch point. After which the whole thing lurched violently to the right, and up a small hill to the hole. This was the kind of hole for which Stroke Indexes[13] were invented. The stream disallowed any notion of skidding a ball across the turf and hoping for an extra 75 yards of progress. You had but one of two choices: lay up or go for it. Laying up, said the Banker, in his habitual mantra, was for pussies, and he was well qualified to know. If the banking community of London, to which he belonged, had decided to 'lay up' in 2008 the world's financial structures might never have collapsed. But they didn't. They just went for glory, landed in the pond, and blew the lot.

I played last, after the other 3 had cleared the obstacle but got themselves into positions of varying difficulty by over-shooting the right hand turn, and rolling into the small

---

[13]A stroke index, surprisingly enough, is nothing to do with a risk factor measurement for heart failure in middle aged men when they find out what they are about to be charged for a round of golf at an elite course. Instead, it numbers, in reverse, what the local committee think is the pecking order difficulty on any given course; 18 being the easiest, and 1 the most difficult. In any bluffer's guide to getting on in golf, discussion of stroke indexes seems to tick many boxes, which is probably why the Cabinet Maker does it with such enthusiasm, bless him.

copse beyond. On a whim, I decided to lay up after all and back myself to get a good second shot in, with a nice angle to the green. Just thinking about 'nice angles to the green', coming from where my own game had come, seemed almost semi-professional, and I went all quiet. A half swing with my 3 wood and the first half of the job was done. The ball bobbled to within about 5 metres of the ditch, more or less exactly where I had wanted it to go.

'You actually played for that, didn't you?' asked the Cabinet Maker, with something as close to admiration as he was prepared to convey. 'You could probably get down in 7 from there, with a bit of luck.'

But I didn't. I fluked a hybrid to the edge of the green, rolled it to within a couple of feet from the hole with a 6 iron, and then sunk it. So much of what normally happened to me on golf courses was accidental, and it was thus a source of amazement to all four of us, in this case, that each of my four shots had done precisely what it had intended to do.

We trudged our way to the 18th tee with more or less everything to play for.

'I bet that's changed your mind about giving it all up after Cornwall,' said the Banker. 'Just look at your smile.'

But it hadn't. He was him, and I was me. I could live for

now in the glory of the minute, but I also knew that the joy I had felt at that last hole would diminish from now on, with each good hole I played. And I knew that the frustration when I played badly would grow in tandem with my body's increasing expectations of itself. Golf was not some zero sum game where it all regulated itself at the end of the year. Most of the golfers I knew well went from trough to trough via occasional peaks, much like the one I had just climbed. Most of them finished each round with a greater sense of regret than they had had to start with. How could the others not see that?

'Roger's honour',[14] said the Cabinet Maker, before adding: 'which must be two of the rarest consecutive words in the English language.'

My confidence was up and I asked to borrow the Banker's diamante-encrusted driver, the first time for at least five years that I had laid my hands on such a potentially unguided missile launcher.[15] I called to mind what the Undergraduate had done with his driver on the range all those months ago, and stepped up to repeat the action. I went through what Tim the Professional had taught me

[14]The 'honour', a peculiar concept that dictates that the last person to win a hole tees off first at the next.
[15]The driver, the largest and most powerful club in the bag, is also the most difficult to control, often spraying the ball 30 degrees or more off line. Hence my self-denying ordinance of the previous five years.

that frosty morning back in Spring. High tee. Wide stance. Left foot opposite the ball. Lean forward. Knees bent. Head slightly tilted to the right. Huge backswing. Weight transfer to the right foot. Swing back. Gather pace. Flick wrists. Strike. Transfer weight onto left foot. Pivot the body. Face down the line of the trajectory. Carefully watch the flight and roll of the ball. Hold the pose. Gradually lower club head. It was all so easy when you knew how.

'It's by your feet,' said the Tree Hugger, helpfully.

'I know it's by my feet,' I said. 'And I'm not taking my trousers down before you ask.'

Somewhere out in the solar system, a blue and green planet continued its rotation, as it had done for 4 billion years, and as it would continue to do for 4 billion more.

Chapter 7

BONDI AND BONDING

An Education Down Under

'*I would rather have bowel surgery in the woods with a stick.
If you are not stung or pronged to death in some unexpected
manner, you may be fatally chomped by sharks or crocodiles,
or carried helplessly out to sea by irresistible currents, or left to
stagger to an unhappy death in the baking outback.*'
Bill Bryson, *In a Sunburned Country*

Experts argue as to whether it is the 2nd or 3rd most
venomous snake on the planet, but, for now at least, the
distinction wasn't of immediate concern to me.

The light brown tail disappearing into the thicket that
contained my mis-driven golf ball belonged to something
that looked very much like *pseudonadia textilis,* or the
Eastern Brown Snake: Taipan to its few friends. I knew
this because I had researched the matter in some depth
before heading Down Under on our long-planned holiday.
'Fast moving, aggressive and known for their bad temper,'
the book had said; 'they are responsible for more deaths

than any other land snake in Australia. Its venom causes progressive paralysis and stops the blood from clotting. Victims may collapse within a few minutes.' Annoyingly, it is also diurnal, much as my golf happens to be, which meant that, for the time being, we were sharing the same workspace.

The Undergraduate and I were all square after 7 of our 9 holes at the Bondi Diggers Club. He had just driven unusually well, whilst I had put my ball, albeit playable, underneath the fringes of a large piece of undergrowth. Back in England, I would have died rather than take a drop and effectively concede the hole but, even with the endless competitive nature of the father son relationship in mind, right now it seemed more likely that I would die if I didn't. I had only spotted the snake as I reached in to get a better look at the ball, and it had left me feeling slightly faint. If it had been small, like an adder, I might have put it down to a trick of the light, but it wasn't. The part of it that I had seen was a good metre long. The inference to this visitor being that it had mammals on the menu, and not necessarily just the tiny ones.

'The Brown Snake occupies a varied range of habitats, from dry forests and the heaths of coastal ranges', the book had said. This place looked like a heath to me. 'It is attracted to farming areas and human habitation due to the large number of assorted rodents'. The fact that only 2 or 3 people die of snake bites in Australia each year was as yet unknown to me, a mystery to be unscrambled in a book I read on the flight home. To be fair to me though, over 50% of them tend to fall victim to an Eastern Brown.

'You going to play?', asked the Undergraduate impatiently, keen to press home his advantage.

'I'm just thinking about my next shot,' I replied. 'I think I'll take a drop'. In my mind's eye I had seen the shiny red and white livery of the New South Wales Air Ambulance parked alongside my convulsing body on the 7th fairway, and I had read the small article on Page 5 of the Times headed, 'Ridiculous British tourist killed by large brown snake on cheap Australian golf course in front of annoying son'. Steve Irwin might well have kissed one of this snake's close relatives on his TV show back in the day, but I was no Steve Irwin, and I was in no mood to become a local statistic. Australia has far more non venomous snakes than venomous, and many of these are brown too, but I wasn't about to take the chance.

We had done British golf. This was Australian golf.

*

The great thing about individual sports is that they are transportable, whereas team sports are not. You can't just turn up in Laos, for example, and expect a game of Rugby Sevens, whereas you *can* go to any of the 204 countries in the world that are equipped with golf courses and reasonably expect to have a round. Golf was not why we had booked a family holiday in Australia, but it seemed unadventurous in the extreme not to at least give it a try now we were here.

We had decided on the 'sublime and ridiculous' approach, playing our first game on an immaculately manicured and exquisitely expensive Country Club course up in Northern Queensland, and our second 1200 miles South in Sydney, at the cheapest club we could find. There wasn't a great deal of doubt in which of these environments we truly belonged, but we like variety in our family and we don't mind chancing our luck. Besides, by the time we got to Sydney, we had blown the holiday budget completely and, in consequence, needed to go for something that cost the same as a burger and chips on the famous beach a couple of hundred feet below where we were currently getting acquainted with the local fauna.

The main issue at The Mirage Country Club in Port Douglas, when the Undergraduate, the Student and I investigated, had more to do with shoes than snakes. The man in the Pro's Shop had been quite voluble on the subject when we went to case the joint the day before.

'We're not very good,' we had told him honestly.

'That's not a problem,' he had replied. 'So long as you have got the right footwear'.

We hadn't. What we had got amounted to what you would bring on a beach holiday with some walking thrown in, punctuated by many trips to the pub. Sandals, sneakers, Timberlands and one pair of trainers between us.

'Is there much water on the course,' I asked.

'Nothing that can't be dealt with in the right shoes,' he came back, cheerfully.

'So we'll go for 11.00 tomorrow,' we said, and he put it in the book.

'Don't forget the shoes,' he called after our retreating forms. In the Mastermind of life, his specialist subject had revealed itself. We were coming to realize that each club had a different priority that they obsessed over. For some it was where you parked your car, just as for others it was a grim determination that no non-member should ever be permitted to set a foot onto their precious course without a guest label on their bag to mark them out as an interloper. Here in North Queensland, it was that visitors played in the right footwear, which, loosely, should be something that looked as if it came out of a golfing catalogue rather than a beach-side kiosk. I never quite understood what the man wanted in respect of our shoes, but I knew full well we couldn't provide it.

The next morning he was ready for us, but then so were

we. As the owner of the nearest footwear we had that would be acceptable to him, I went in to the shop to pay, and the others tried their hardest to look busy and competent outside the window, feet hidden from view. Classically attired club members moved among us with confidence, their very correctness depressing in itself. With horror I noticed that the form he gave me to fill in and sign included an official box next to each of the signatures saying, 'Footwear approved', with a space for him to tick.

A telephone call diverted him and drew him to an adjacent room, and then into a rather involved conversation about sandwiches, or sand wedges, the accent made it difficult to work out which. But he was gone for enough time for his assistant to offer to complete the process of our temporary enrolment and for me to tick all 3 'footwear approved' boxes before she came over. The issue was a continuation of a theme running through my early golf career that ensured that, however much I had tried to turn up in acceptable kit, I was destined always to be one stage below the required standard on the day.

Only as I turned in to sleep that evening did it occur to me that this was the first time, with the possible exception of our trip to Inner London, when the likely quality of my golf wasn't the only issue on my mind on arriving at a smart club. I had played enough games by now to be relatively confident that I could organize my various muscle groups to do roughly what I wanted them to on the same number of occasions as they didn't. A challenging course no longer terrorized me as it had 6 months ago; it just intrigued me. It no longer stunned me if I got down a hole in par, or went round a sequence of three holes in no more than 3 over, and I had developed some vestige of ability to pull an awful round out of the fire before it was too late. In some spectacularly modest way, I was becoming a golfer, even though I still lacked the diamond patterned Pringle sweater and the weird obsession with hierarchy and rules.

In the event, the course might have been a bit of a disappointment, were it not for one thing. In pure golfing terms, the short rough, the environment in which I happen to play much of my golf, consisted of a native breed of grass so tough and wiry that it was almost impossible to maintain any club head speed or direction through it. The bunkers, the habitat that the Student traditionally makes all his own on his rare forays into the sport, were iron hard and prodigious in number. The greens, those hallowed places we all dream of arriving at eventually, seemed to have been coated in a thin veneer of wood glue and almost needed a half swing of a hybrid club to move the ball any distance across it.

The saving grace was water. Lots and lots of water. Hole after hole of wet obstacles, deep ponds, streams, creeks and ditches. The back nine in particular, which runs along the north side of Port Douglas' peninsula, is akin to a manicured mangrove swamp and, here in North

Queensland, swamps mean fish and fish mean crocodiles. All the water obstacles had bright yellow warning signs with red writing advising us how to mix with our indigenous neighbours or, more accurately, how not to. The cartoon crocodile depicted on each of these signs looked more friendly than ferocious, its mouth half open in the form of a welcoming smile. 'Come and have a dip when you get too hot,' it seemed to be saying. 'Just like I am'.

What had directed our choice of courses was nothing to do with the quality of the sport it afforded, but the discovery that Mirage Country Club boasted at least a dozen resident salt water crocodiles. The previous October, a friendly 3.6 metre specimen had been removed and sent to a local game reserve on the basis that he was beginning to become a bit too relaxed among the golfers, as they had been around him, and a collision of some sort seemed increasingly likely. What our golf needed, we felt, was the spice and adventure that only the presence of a potentially lethal reptile could truly offer. Besides, it was an opportunity to get one over on the Cabinet Maker, whose much-vaunted and ruinously expensive round at Banff in Canada earlier in the summer had failed to produce so much as a moose, let alone the Grizzly he had been promised. Keen to rub it in, I had texted him our plans the evening before.

'I hope something eats you,' he had replied overnight, *'before you bore it to death'*.

*

The whole point of playing a sport abroad is that it is better in every way than playing at home.

Euclid's 3rd Law of Inverse Anticipation dictates, of course, that the expectations of your own skill and competence rise both with the beauty of the course and with the growing distance from home. Since the Mirage was a very beautiful course, and we were about as far from home as we could be without putting on a space suit, the three of us harboured sky high ambitions on this bright Tuesday morning. The 100 yard ponds looked carry-able, the deep bunkers escapable and the fairways attractively drive-able. The tedious truth lies, however, in the opposite direction: whilst you will thrive on a grim council course on the outskirts of a complex of disused coal mines in a grey and rain-swept Welsh Valley, in a place like Mirage you will routinely fall to pieces. And if you don't, I will.

For the first few holes we saw nothing of note, so I quietly bird-watched between shots whilst the Student and the Undergraduate behaved like delinquents in our buggy. For 35 years I have found that bird-watching is like a cheap version of golf in that you can be bad at it almost anywhere in the world, and can even alter the score card at the end of the game if it means that much to you. All you need is a pair of binoculars, the local bird book, and a personality that hovers somewhere on the spectrum between tragic and unfriendable. The joy of a good, confirmed spot to a birdwatcher is not unlike a decent 120 yard pitch to the heart of the green, other than it costs a lot less and can be done in almost any type of footwear. Besides, you don't have to join a club and be told how to behave in ornithology: you just look at stupid things with wings and they, in turn, look back at you. They don't bark orders at you, or exclude you from the captain's table. They don't elect club officers and glare at younger members through the bitterness of age. They just fly around looking pretty, and lay eggs.

A cute little black and white Willie Wagtail lurked on a branch near the eleventh tee.

An aboriginal guide had told us a little earlier that we had to be quiet when a Willie Wagtail was nearby or else it would tell our secrets to the spirits, particularly if we were speaking badly of them. In the event the only secrets that this particular bird would have been able to take back to its spirit masters was that the Undergraduate had shanked his drive violently into the adjoining creek, and that he had called the Student a 'wanker' for laughing at it. He might also have pointed out that there was a threesome of locals just behind us, tea-potting just enough to make the unsubtle point that they would like to play through, and do so soon.

We duly invited them to and watched them pass

thanklessly to the next tee; two weather-beaten Aussie men and a huge Aussie woman. The latter glared at us as if someone had just farted.

'You beautiful bastard!' said the first as his ball described an elegant 200 yard parabola towards the green.

'Piece of piss,' said the second when he had hit his in similar fashion, adding 'Ratbag' as an unconnected after-thought. They made way for the huge woman who duly addressed her ball on the lady's tee 20 or so yards further on, and proceeded to top it with rich venom into the pond in front.

'Fucking Drongo,' she mouthed, as her ball disappeared into the mangrove ecosystem. 'Fuck this. I'm done.' And, pausing briefly to glare at the three of us behind her as if it was all our fault, she stomped her way back to the club house and the 32 ounce chuck steak that beckoned from beyond her horizon.

By the time we had come to the last hole we had seen but one small and wholly inoffensive crocodile. It was swimming in the opposite direction from us with the faint apologetic air of a man who had just walked into the girls' changing room and was back-tracking as unobtrusively as possible. We felt rather cheated, to be honest. Our golf had veered between acceptable and ridiculous, as it always seemed to, but golf somehow wasn't the entire point of the day. This animal sighting was a small footnote in the notes of a nature ramble, but not the life event we had been banking on.

Like so many final holes, the 18th at Mirage manages to look like an afterthought, an uneasy last minute connection between the 17 holes that preceded it and the clubhouse a couple of hundred yards away. With a large reservoir running along the left side, and thick undergrowth on the right, it was tailor-made for a homicidal drive from each of us, on the basis that surely one of the three would make it all the way to the green. A couple of groundsmen had parked their buggy 100 yards down the fairway and had stopped what they were doing to watch keenly for how we got on.

In our differing ways, we can all hit a golf ball quite hard when the moon is in our star sign and, occasionally, we can hit it both hard and accurately. The Undergraduate has been known to drive nearly 300 yards on his day, but this was not to be one of them. Not for him or for either of his companions.

One of the small tragedies ever-present in the life of the developing golfer happens to be the very public shortness of his or her walk from the tee to the first resting place of their ball after its initial drive. Skilled golfers stride off from the tee as if equipped for a long expedition, enough time on their hands before their next shot to discuss

Nietzsche's genealogical critique of Christian ethics, or to recite the first 500 lines or so of Beowulf. There is no limit as to what can be intellectually achieved by someone on a long walk. The rookie golfer, on the other hand, has hardly started the process of putting one foot in front of another when he is having to slow down in readiness for his next shot, a phenomenon exaggerated further if he has hired a buggy for the round, and yet more humiliating if he is close to a centre of population, like the first tee. If he were to try to start up a conversation, it would need to be about the shortest and most discrete of subjects, like an Israeli knock-knock joke, or a list of Indian Olympic legends. On this occasion, and having planned the long and invigorating walk, all 3 of us scuffed our drives into the near middle distance, 100 yards or so from where we stood and right in front of the appreciative gazes of the green-keepers.

It took us a mere 30 seconds to reach the general area of our balls. We decanted ourselves onto the fairway hoping that raucous laughter on our part would give the impression that we were having a joke hole, and had all driven off with a putter, rather than that we were just useless at this game.

'Aren't you going to say "hello" to your new friend, then?' said one of the spectators.

Thinking that we were being pulled up for a lack of

manners, I duly said 'hello' to them, as did the Student and Undergraduate.

'Not us,' he continued, 'the other one behind you.'

We looked, and there, 10 yards to the front and left of my ball relaxed a beautiful 4 metre crocodile,[16] mouth half open to cool down rather than to eat, and motionless except the fathomless eye that now watched for how my second shot would go.

'Hello,' I said rather weakly, but within my chest my heart was singing. On the basis that it didn't eat one of us, which on the face of it was unlikely, its appearance as an obstacle was of itself sufficient success for the round.

I addressed the ball, choosing a 9 iron to combine loft with sufficient potential distance not to need to disturb it again on its other side. The ball duly soared over the animal, and parked itself somewhere in the vicinity of the green. Job done, even if the crocodile seemed unimpressed. The Student did much the same thing, but with a pitching wedge and a slightly more elegant result. But, when the Undergraduate came to play his ball, he chose a sand

---

[16]*Crocodylus porosus*, which belongs to the 'be careful what you wish for' section of animal conservation. By 1974, they had become strictly protected all over Australia, unlike people who waded, swum or fished near them, who hadn't.

wedge, which pivoted the ball 30 yards almost vertically up in the air before it came to rest a metre or two to the north-east of the business end of the crocodile.

The Undergraduate was one up, with one to play, so to claim a drop at this point was an almost certain concession of the hole and therefore the round. He then made the basic error of believing that family love, coupled with a father's protective instinct, would triumph over the underlying competitive imperative.

'Can I take a free drop?' he asked, pathetically. We sensed that this was to be his last honeyed verbal offering before it got nasty.

'Is it a man-made hazard?' I replied.

'What's that got to do with anything? he asked.

'Because if it is, then no problem.' Rules 24 and 25 of the Royal and Ancient are quite clear on the subject: 'an immovable obstruction is an artificial object on the course that cannot be moved (e.g a building) or cannot be readily moved (e.g a firmly embedded direction post).'

'But you know it bloody isn't; it's a fucking salt-water crocodile, and I'm your son. Do you really want me to get eaten by it?'

I mulled this question over.

'It's resting,' said the Student thoughtfully. 'It might not eat you'. As a student of philosophy it was hard to argue with his comment.

'He's right,' I added. 'You could probably stroke it right now, and not be inconvenienced.'

At this point the Green Keepers intervened, helpfully as it turned out. They confirmed that, as it didn't constitute a man-made hazard of itself, the ball would have to be played *in situ*.

Bravado and cowardice are uneasy bedfellows, but the Undergraduate displayed them both. He took about 5 determined steps towards the crocodile, confident that it would think better of any altercation, as most wildlife tends to, and slip back into the reservoir. It didn't. Instead, it gave him a lingering look that suggested that it thought a 9 iron would have been a better choice, and that he lacked manners. It moved its tail imperceptibly, and blinked one of its 3 eyelids in a fashion that denoted complete, if critical, calm.

One more despairing look at the Student and me followed and then, amid a chorus of 'fucks', and much, much worse, he played his 4th shot from a drop and left his brand new monogrammed Callaway 4 to a resident of the dinosaur era.

Never had a round been more beautifully squared.

*

Two weeks later, and on our last afternoon in Australia, I had a dilemma. We were in Sydney and I was still 11 short of my target of 200 newly identified bird species, meaning that I really needed to be ferreting around by rock pools and urban gardens, rather than playing golf.

'Bondi will be full of bloody birds,' said the Undergraduate enthusiastically, not quite understanding my dilemma, or the kinds of bird that I was after. 'Besides, the round will only cost us $15, which will end up cheaper than sitting in this pub'.

The Student excused himself. Having rediscovered wi-fi for the first time in a week he had important and urgent bonding to do with his 850 Facebook friends in their beds all those thousands of miles away under leaden English skies.

'Can I help you?,' said the Pro, in a way that made us feel that we had disturbed the tranquility of his otherwise perfect Wednesday afternoon. Unusually for a golf Pro, he was dressed as for a ju-jitsu match, in a loose white martial arts suit with black belt.

'Nine holes for two, and the cheapest clubs you've got. And, by the way, is that thing on the terrace a Variegated Fairy Wren do you know?'

He looked at the Undergraduate, and then gave me a look that indicated he thought I should be on the Sex Offenders Register.

'No, the bird. That one with his tail up.'

'$30 for the 2 rounds and $20 for the clubs. You want balls? I'll throw in 4'. Translated into English, what he meant was 'please get out of my life, and only come back in when something has eaten you'.

Bondi's opening hole is, at 145 yards, the longest of the first 4, and the Undergraduate duly struck his 7 iron tee shot 50 yards too far and to the cliff edge beyond.

His golf is, at the best of times, the nearest thing I know to a piece of unexploded ordnance, or an unbroken stallion. The club quivers in his hands in his preparation for the shot, a reservoir of untapped kinetic energy about to be released once and for all into the community. His backswing has the look of a giant and dangerous spring being wound to its limit. Whereas others will lay their ball up with great subtlety on the fringes of the green for the measured approach shot, the Undergraduate will take it as a personal insult if he hasn't cleared the hole by the length of 2 cricket pitches, and snapped his tee in two in the process. Years of sporting failure at his various schools have produced in him the notion that an under hit shot is an insult to his manhood, and that a lay-up is unacceptable under any circumstances. If my golf belongs to the pages of *Saga*, and it probably does, his is *Hustler* with a dash of *Men's Health* thrown in for good measure, and it is occasionally more awesome than effective. His magnificent driving enjoys a similar success rate to the last ten England football managers, albeit minus the sleaze, the shagging, the excuses and the petty corruption.

My own opening shot was more controlled, and, by a series of slightly interconnected flukes, bounces and deviations, arrived on the green in a fashion that meant that even someone of extraordinary incompetence would fail to put down in par. The fact that I went down in a further 5 shots I put down partly to the lunar surface of the green, and partly to the arrival in a neighbouring bit of scrub of Bird number 191, a White-throated Honeyeater. Or at least I thought it was a White Throated Honeyeater, but they are easily confused from a distance with White Naped Honeyeaters, with whom they often flock.[17] This meant I needed to get both the binoculars out of the bag

[17] I can tell you were worried. It was a White Naped Honeyeater, as it had an orange eye crescent. More importantly, I needed one, whereas I had already seen the White Throated version.

to get a good view of its markings, and my glasses out of my pocket in order to then compare the details in the book. Bird-watching had been a darn sight easier 30 years before, when most of the component parts of my body still worked.

We steadily worked our way round the holes. Two bogeys and a Pied Currawong (192) on the second. A par, a bogey and a compliment from a confused golfer who appeared to be doing the course backwards, on the 121 yard third. A lost ball on the fourth, but a Little Lorikeet (193) in the bag for my efforts, and an idle chance to watch the surfers on the celebrated beach down below. Another pair of bogeys on the 6th, plus a chance to see and smell Bondi's main sewage treatment works, which kind of explained why there so many bird number 194s (Crested Pigeon) milling about, as the stools of the surfing community were processed into something altogether more wholesome and agreeable.

By the time we got to the 7th, with its resident Taipan, thirst, the long trip and the growing awareness of suit-cases to pack had got the better of us, and we quickly polished off the next 2 holes (all square, plus Australian Raven (195)). The Undergraduate had come back from a poor start to square the match, and my bird list was close enough to the magic 200 for me to be able to pretend it didn't matter. The other 5 could be added somehow in the long flight to Hong Kong that evening.

*

An idle thought passed between us as we strolled back down the steep hill to what passed as Bondi's clubhouse, and not for the first time: this irritating, frustrating, magnificent game could be perfection, even among idiots, even on one of the most basic courses in the Southern Hemisphere, so long as you were in a nice place and the idiot you were with was one you quite liked. Actually, you didn't even need to be in a nice place.

'Thanks, Dad,' said the Undergraduate.

'What for?' I asked, knowing that we had shared the expense of the round together, and that Undergraduates generally thank as a prelude to a financial request.

'Doing stuff like this with me'.

It was one of those little bits of magic that life throws up from time to time, and it had all cost no more than $15.00 a head. Fathers spend endless years wanting to hear a comment like this, and then milliseconds not knowing how to react gracefully or correctly.

'Twat,' I said as kindly as I could as we handed our clubs back in at the shop.

'Git,' he replied, and we headed off to fly home to a land where crocodiles lived in zoos, and where the most venomous snake around only gives you a slightly sore foot if it bites you.

Chapter 8

THE DARK NIGHT OF THE HOLE

Implosion

'I have not failed. I've just found 10,000 ways that won't work.'
Thomas A Edison

On September 24th, at 17 minutes past 9 in the morning, it all fell apart, and all because of an elephant.

To be fair, I had been waiting for it to crumble. As the year had progressed, my game became little by little more competent, and rather more acceptable in public. A 200 yard drive was no longer a once-in-a-round event, and the same could be said for dinky little approach shots and 6 foot putts. Granted, I was progressing less surely than the Cabinet Maker, less elegantly than the Banker and less violently than the Undergraduate, but I was progressing nonetheless. That magical moment in a golfer's career had arrived wherein the ring of bunkers protecting a hole could be viewed more as a challenge and less as a terrorist plot.

The elephant, the one that had hitherto been quietly hiding behind the sofa and had now emerged trumpeting into the room, was my utter lack of sustainable technique. My swing, rather than being an effortlessly repeatable sequence of planned biometric actions, was merely derived from a thousands bits of random muscle memory coupled with a pathological need not to get beaten by someone called Trevor. That was it. So long as the sun shone in my firmament, it did what it was fundamentally supposed to do. But, when the clouds of self-destruction rolled in, it had nowhere to go, no umbrella to hoist, no metaphorical clubhouse to retreat to.

My drive off the first tee that September morning flattered to deceive, but it was the last thing that did. Full of false confidence and a minor skin full of San Miguel from the previous night, I opted for a hybrid for my fairway shot. It was not a good choice that early in the round, and the ball duly scooted off into the short rough to my left. I ignored the Cabinet Maker's barbs and addressed the ball again, this time with a 3 wood. The ball, tiring of the short rough, ploughed deeper into the longer stuff even further to its left. A calming pause would have been the mature action at that moment, but my maturity was lying in the long rough with my golf ball, wetting itself at the situation I was in.

'Still you,' said the Cabinet Maker, helpfully.[18]

[18]Another of golf's little etiquettes is that the player furthest from the hole always plays next. Which means that if you play twice running, you have probably done something awful. Wits like the Cabinet Maker make dead sheep ('still ewe') noises, and how we all laugh.

Deep in the dark recesses of my brain, someone pulled one of those giant red mains switches marked 'Plot, losing the...' and I executed another homicidal attack on the ball with the 3 wood. Vegetation went everywhere, but the ball stayed more or less where it was.

'You again?' said the Cabinet Maker.

I flung the 3 wood back in my bag and pulled out my late father's old 7 wood rescue club. Its smaller head, and greater concentration of weight in the right place would get me back in business and on the fringe of the green. It didn't. It got me 120 yards across the fairway, into an area of dried mud that was not really in bounds, but not really out of it. When I got there, and out of the corner of my eye, I noticed a warty toad leaving the scene.

At this point, there were a number of battles taking place within the warzone that my body had become. The first was a simple struggle not to weep at the implosion of something that had held so much promise only minutes before, and to which disaster had come so early in the round. This was shortly followed by a more traditional fight not to commit a sudden and random act of violence on my crowing opponent. That one, in turn, was escorted from the premises by a complete amnesia as to what I should, or even could, do next in order to extricate myself from the metaphorical hole I was in. The final one was a middle-class, middle-aged, middle English determination not to be seen to be losing it, or even remotely inconvenienced by it, whatever '*it*' was. The resulting contortion was not pretty, and it was no basis for a renaissance in my game.

'Take your time,' said the Cabinet Maker, before adding that, on second thoughts, it wouldn't make a jot of difference to my situation if I took till Lammas Night to prepare for the next shot.

I addressed the ball once more, this time with a 7 iron, and tried to rack my brain for what Tim, the Professional, might say if he were standing opposite me as he had done during those long-lost lessons at the driving range. Never in my life had I wanted more to be in the company of someone called Tim. Any Tim would have done at this stage. Rice, Henman, Brook-Taylor, West, anyone.

First, he would have told me to relax, and to envisage the ball going precisely where I wanted it to. This was tricky as I wasn't entirely sure where I wanted the ball to go. 'On the green' tied with 'in the Cabinet Maker's anal passage' as a preferred destination, so I moved on to the next one.

Then he would have told me to line my feet up either side of the ball, lay my club down behind it, lean slightly forwards, bend my knees a little, and begin a slow, smooth backswing, during which my weight would transfer gently to my right foot, which would remain nonetheless planted fully on the ground. I did so.

After this, he would have told me to envisage the great circle of the club's swing, and to imagine at what point in that circle the club head would make sweet, sweet contact with the ball below; keeping my head still and my eyes on the ball all the while. Again, I did so.

Then he would have urged me to let the momentum of that balanced swing carry my upper body smoothly round to the left, until it was facing immediately down the course towards the green, right leg pivoting round, and right heel 4 inches above the ground. Then I should just watch the ball rise true and straight into the late summer morning on its way to the edge of the green. I did that, too. I did all these things in the way that I had been taught, and in the grim belief that they would of themselves override the red switch that had been thrown only minutes before.

They didn't. The ball did at least head for a short distance in the vague direction of the green, but the cataclysm of my still young round had completely disenabled the other me, that affable and confident me that had last been seen climbing out of his car not half an hour before thoroughly looking forward to a game of golf. That man was now but a distant memory. I only knew quite how badly it was going when the Cabinet Maker stopped being rude, and started feeling sorry for me. 'Sympathy', as a former Canadian Army colleague had once explained to a gang of us on an exercise in Germany, comes in the sporting dictionary somewhere between 'Shit' and 'Syphilis'.

Things were bad, true enough, but they would have to be ethnically-cleansing bad before I needed the emotional consideration of the Cabinet Maker.

*

In the end I got round, but I was a broken man.

For 8 of the 9 holes, the fragments of my game assembled themselves on each tee, before disintegrating on the way to the next hole. On the 9th, I unfurled a drive that was at least recognizable as a distant relative of the game of golf that I had come to expect to play these days, but I suspected it was yet another false dawn. The inherent vulnerability of both my technique and temperament was a powerful force indeed, and I knew that something far more significant than just a bad round of golf had just taken place. Once it was over, it was all I could do to climb in my car and go home. I couldn't even bring myself to stop at the café and share a habitual coffee with my friend.

'It doesn't matter,' I kept telling myself through gritted teeth. 'It's only a game.' But this was merely the golfing equivalent of my parents telling the boyhood me that some hungry child elsewhere in the world would be grate- ful for what I was leaving on my plate – theoretically true, but utterly irrelevant. I was fairly and squarely in the zone within which seemingly rational grown men hurl their complete golf bag and contents into the pond, or at least into the local Cancer Research Shop.

I stared at the calm waters of the River Rother as I drove over Coultershaw Bridge on my way back from the game, and pondered for a minute as I was held up by an approaching combine harvester that filled the narrow roadway, what an excellent memorial to the stupidity of adult sport my clubs and bag would look, parked provocatively where the Mute Swans nest on the sandy island, just upstream from where the A272 crossed. In modern parlance, it would pass as a sophisticated art installation, one that helped define man's place in the Universe, and I felt sure I could persuade the Arts man with the funny hair from the BBC to cover it for *Front Row* in due course. I would be interviewed, obviously, and would be invited to those North London dinners where comfortably left-wing men wear cravats and waistcoats, use cocaine, and utter the words '*really significant*' often, and with real meaning. There would be articles in the Sunday Times Magazine about how I, among *avante garde* artists, best understood the human condition, and was therefore culturally important. Possibly, I would be invited to be a panelist on *In Our Time* by Melvyn Bragg, possibly not. I was woken from this daydream when a lad in a pimped up azure Ford Focus behind me angrily hooted his two-tone horn in his pathetic attempt to get to his appointment at the Acne Clinic six seconds earlier than he otherwise would have. In a way, his intervention summed my problem up rather neatly: at this precise moment, I wasn't even very good at not being very good at something.

I played someone else one evening that week, and the same thing happened. I went out on my own the following morning, long before the course had opened for business, to see if it would change things if I removed the pressure of competition and just concentrated on doing what I had been taught. It didn't, because I couldn't. And I couldn't because, deep down, the fragility of my game mirrored some fragility in my psychological make-up; that part of my brain marked 'self-belief'. Besides, I was saying 'fuck' a lot, and it was only a matter of time before I said it in front of the Lady Captain or a passing Imam.

To my eternal shame, I took it out on the Banker and the Cabinet Maker, the two friends who I had originally dragged into golf, and whose only fault was to be better, and calmer, and more consistent than me. I started by finding a reason why I couldn't play the following week-end, or the one after that. When their pressure persisted, I failed to return calls. And when the Banker finally cornered me on the subject in the local wine bar, I told him that I was giving it up for a year, if not for ever.

'Why?', he said. 'Your game will come back. And, isn't it enough just to be out there with your mates?'

'Sorry,' I said, 'I'm just not enjoying it'. But what I really meant was that I was just not enjoying them being better than me.

'But we have fun, don't we? I mean, golf or no golf. You're the reason why we all started this, and you can't stop it now.'

'Sorry, David,' I said, 'it's over'. I was being an utter tool, but I secretly liked the bit about me being the reason we had all started it.

'Oh well,' he said. 'It's your decision. It's just a bit of a shame that your book will never see the light of day.'

The book. I hadn't thought about the book.

*

That book.

Half a decade before, I had written another book, this one about a cricket team, but that had been so very different. First, it was a joint undertaking with a friend; secondly, it was about a game that I loved, and whose every twist and turn was familiar to me; and finally, it was historical, featuring stuff that had happened, often years before, and simply needed an activated memory, or at least imagination, to release onto paper. My current golf project was different in every respect: it was a solo effort, about a game that I hardly knew, and about which I had very mixed feelings, and it was all in the future. When I embarked on it I had no idea how it would unfold. It was a leap into the unknown, and it didn't necessarily have to end well.

The Germans call it *torschlusspanik:* the fear that life's opportunities are closing off one by one with the passing years, like hinged gates. That, in the end, is why I had taken up this game. And it was why I had decided to write a book about it. Somewhere deep within me, I just didn't want to risk the chance of shuffling off this mortal coil not having tried as many things as I could off the a la carte menu of my leisure time. Golf loomed large because people around me did lots of it; they talked about it and reminisced over it like I did over cricket, and many of them were manifestly good at it. In much the same way that one has no real choice over the identity of the crap football team one spends a lifetime supporting as one is just born with it, golf for me turned out to be an inevitability and nothing to do with adult choice. This, if anything, made my body's refusal to be any good at it even more galling.

What had startled me was the inescapability of golf, and its recent permanence as a feature of my life. Cricket is something I do maybe 15 times each year between early May and mid September. Success or failure depends on the combined efforts of all 11 players and thus the dropped catch, or the dubious LBW decision, can be rationalized away in the warm glow of victory in the pub afterward, or at least in the warm glow of having had a nice day in the sunshine with friends, if the result had gone the wrong way.

Golf, on the other hand, stalks you like an unloved dog

that an unloved aunt has asked you to look after while she is away in an unloved health resort. The week's routine can easily be lived in its shadow, bad shots repeating themselves in your mind as if on catch-up TV, and the inevitability of collapse trotting on to the First Tee beside you, wagging its stupid, pointless little tail and lifting its leg on the tee box. Or, worse still, on your golf bag. Except on the rare occasion when fate intervenes, usefully or viciously, everything that happens in that 3 hour, 4 mile walk, is down to the individual player. His or her inner battles are visible, public and hideously personal. It is quite simply you, a club and a ball, and what happens happens. Unlike nearly any other sport, it cannot subsequently be blamed on appalling umpiring decisions, team or equipment failure, deteriorating weather conditions or a team manager's misplaced decision to change from wets to slicks mid-race.

Two of my previous sporting careers (rugby union and boxing) had ended respectively on a stretcher and in the A and E department of a South West England hospital; one (rock climbing) should have, and would have had there been a hospital within 40 miles of the Cuillin Ridge on the Isle of Skye that I fell off, and one (squash) ended as a thoroughly thumped quarter finalist in a tournament, in the course of which I had received no less than 3 byes on my way to that exalted round. But the pain of injury and concussion is nothing, let me tell you, in comparison to the relentless draining effect of under-achievement at golf. On each occasion that your ball is sliced, hooked or chopped into the surrounding forestry, a little bit of you dies. And, if you do that often, like I do, there comes a time when there are no original bits left to die. You wake one morning to become the mental embodiment of the Paradox of Theseus' Ship[19]: a sporting zombie with new bits harvested from the long dead.

The crash in form hit the rest of my life as well. I would like to have thought that, at the age of 56, I would have learned how to rationalize the slings and arrows of outrageous fortune that visited the little part of my life that golf comprised, but I was wrong. I still theoretically enjoyed the band-of-brothers that we had long been, but the thought that I was fated to evermore be the joker, the fall guy who could be relied on to make everyone happy as he thrashed around each course we played, hurt like hell. And I knew in my heart of hearts that it would only get worse from here on: the others would go on getting better, ticking off the little milestones in their progress towards buying Rovers and little woolen club cozies; lowering their handicaps whilst I couldn't even get one. Just because I was failing to keep up didn't actually mean that I took any pleasure in lagging behind. I had my pride, even if it was entirely misplaced.

[19]A thought experiment that questions whether something that has had all its component replaced is still fundamentally the same thing. Like the Labour Party, or Dolly Parton's breasts.

I grew to realize that golf can be the loneliest place in the sporting firmament when it goes wrong, and my game had gone very, very wrong. If it was still depressing me as much as it had been that Saturday morning when it fell apart, it would not be so much a fit of pique to pack it in, but a rational and kindly action in an uncertain world. I said as much to the Cabinet Maker when I saw him in the coffee bar, and, for a change, he thought it all through before he gave me his considered reply.

'Utter bollocks,' he said, 'Man up and stop being a git.' He made it clear that neither he or the Banker were going to stop just because I had and that, when the Undergraduate came down from University, they would have no problem replacing me in the foursome with someone made of sterner stuff. He looked at me sadly for a while and then said;

'It's not about you, you know. It's about us. You're the only one that notices when it all goes tits up. The rest of us just plod round and think you're having fun, like we are. We just like being with you, whatever your golf is like.'

It was the nicest speech he had made to me for years, and I could tell that he minded, that I was hurting.

'Besides,' he added, 'If you quit, we can't play at South-downs any more, and then we'll have to join'. He paused for a second or two for effect. 'And I suppose it proves that the Secretary down in Cornwall has had the last laugh. That he was right all along.'

Which turned out to be what I needed to get going again, and Tim in consequence got the long overdue call.

*

Tim had an effect, as he always does, but it was one particular shot that changed the direction of travel. One little shot.

And sometimes in life, one single random success, one thing not going ball-grindingly wrong, is all it takes to change direction. It might be something at work for which you are erroneously credited, but permanently changes management's opinion of you; or an opponent landing on Vine Street, when Vine Street has the only hotel you own on the Monopoly Board, among all your sad and mortgaged properties. The point is that it creates momentum, and momentum is the undefinable force that releases you from your exoskeleton of mediocrity. The seesaw of life moves fractionally along the fulcrum and, in consequence, instead of knowing that what you are about to do is going to go wrong for the umpteenth time, a tiny part of your brain suggests that maybe it might just go right.

I was in a bunker beside and below the second hole at Southdowns, and had had to borrow a sand wedge, because some previous depression and underachievement had caused me to leave my own in some distant sand trap weeks before. I knew but three things: first, plant your feet firmly in the sand so as to get a good base; second, hit a point an inch behind the ball and third, follow through for all you are worth. I took my time, and tried to do each of them. But this time, instead of going vertically up in the air and then coming to rest exactly where it had been before; instead of firing itself into the hard bank of the bunker and skewing off into an even worse lie, or drill itself on the full 85 yards into the copse the other side of the pin, it did something odd. It rose lazily in a plume of sand from where it lay, landed half way to the pin, and then rolled slowly, directly, to a spot 18 inches from the hole. This was what they did on the telly, only without the stupid hats and annoying towel-holding caddies. My reaction to rare moments of sporting excellence – the back-hand intercept at the tennis net, for example, or the diving slip catch – is to go silent. I have worked out that I do this for a conscious reason (I just might be 'in the zone' for the first time in my life and I don't want to spoil it), and a sub-conscious one (my brain doesn't know how to react to such success). The effect of my shot, and the ensuing silence, on the Cabinet Maker and the Banker was complex, schizophrenic even. Every sinew within them wanted to minimize whatever advantage I had gained from what had happened. However, weighing against that neolithic urge, some small and decent part of each of them was just glad to have their mate back.

Eventually, my opponents were generous in their comments, possibly because they preferred the cocky me to the miserable, whining idiot they had been tolerating when things weren't going his way.

'Is that a Gimme?' I asked.

'In your dreams,' said the Banker with feeling. 'You've missed shorter putts than that. Often.'

I putted out to win the hole. I was back.

Chapter 9

GEAR AND CLOTHING IN SEATTLE

A Round in the Pacific North West

'Go play golf. Go to the golf course. Hit the ball. Find the ball. Repeat until the ball is in the hole. Repeat this 18 times. Have fun. The end.'
Chuck Hogan, *U.S. writer*

At 2.45 in the morning Eastern Standard Time on November 9th 2016, the world as we knew it convulsed with the election of Donald J Trump as the 45th President of the USA. In this year of surprises, from the British electorate's decision that they were fed up with being second guessed by their Oxbridge leaders, to the death of the *Space Oddity*, this was possibly the biggest of all.

The week after his election coincided with my return trip to see David in Seattle, a liberal-minded city which, given it had voted about 80% for Clinton, was in the deepest of deep mourning. As I reached my hotel to check in, a small group of students were singing 'We Shall Overcome' on the pavement outside, without the faintest shred of conviction, and below a banner which enigmatically read

'Not in my name'. I tried to say something encouraging as I passed by, but I was old and old people like me had just buggered up their world, and they just looked at me with liberal contempt. Anyone who has been stared down by a grieving liberal student with contempt will know roughly what I had to pass through. I paused briefly to try to parade some innate liberal credentials, like a mother might show off an ugly newborn baby, but a student who looked far too healthy and prosperous to be on a picket line indicated with her middle finger that the interview was over.

I was a child of the sixties for whom America meant John Wayne, big hats and Cadillacs. There was nothing complicated about the role the Americans had in our lives: they ran them, and frankly, we admired them for it. Their Presidents flickered onto our screens in black and white saying the same kind of weighty things about the world we lived in that our parents routinely said on a much smaller scale about our homes and schools. Everything about their country was bigger and better than ours: the buildings were higher, the bridges longer, the teeth whiter and, according to my *Ladybird Book of the USA*, you could drive straight through the middle of trees in one of their national parks. This was before it all got complicated by oil, religion and guns. It was a giant pastureland, where the only Donald that we had heard of was a blameless duck. Our biggest criticism of the Americans in those faraway, innocent days was that they tended to turn up for major conflicts after the half time whistle had been blown.

I had played golf in the USA once before, a quarter of a century ago, at the Tater Hill Country Club in Vermont's Okemo Mountain. It was during the one business trip my father and I ever did together, and about a year before he died. Being a great stage manager, his motivation for the few days off we took in New England was to give me the kind of long-term life advice that a father can't hand over to a son during a trip down to the local pub for a quick pint. Being a great evader of advice, my own motivation was to make it almost impossible for him to give any by keeping him too busy in boyish activities to get enough momentum to do so.

But, it was in the Clubhouse of Tater Hill that he casually told me over a beer that he was dying, (something I instinctively knew anyway), so the prospect of US golf still tends to cast long shadows across my memory all these years later. That evening, for the first and last time, we got drunk together. It was in Manchester, Vermont and it ended with us finally having to be shown out of the little clapperboard restaurant when the owners wanted to go to sleep, and then briefly forgetting where our hotel was. We giggled at our predicament on the pavement outside, and probably nearly even hugged each other. The odd thing was that, although he never got round to giving his advice, I knew what it would be all along, and I rather regret not having given him the opportunity. I would have ignored it, just like my sons will ignore mine, but it would have given him pleasure to have delivered it.

*

Twenty years on, and six months after his visit to the UK, David would have felt himself justified in thinking that my golf would have improved to a point that I could keep my end up at the Seattle Golf Club.

'Dude,' he had said on his email the week before, 'We'll go play some golf at my club, so bring some clothes.'

I would have been more relaxed if I hadn't decided to Google 'Seattle Golf Club' a week or so before the trip.

Arnold Palmer himself apparently described it as, 'one of the most outstanding courses in the Northwest, if not the nation' (admittedly shortly before he was awarded the contract for redesigning it). The Club's own website mentioned that it 'invites the technical and thoughtful golfer to not only admire the course's spectacular beauty, but to test his or her skills against the narrow fairways and speedy greens'. 'Technical', 'thoughtful', 'narrow' and 'speedy' were not adjectives that would leap into the front rank of my wish list of potential venues. I was more of a 'easy', 'gentle', 'wide' and 'slow' man myself, with a hint of 'ironic' thrown in for good measure at the end. The clubhouse, when it loomed into view between the massive

Douglas Firs and Sitka Spruces of the approach, looked like a scene from Gatsby, completing the impression that this was by far the most grown up course I had ever inflicted my game on. There was something about the manicured excellence of it all that suggested that I, and my game, was about to be seen through in a big, big way.

Being generally indifferent at technical things has taught me not to be a particularly nervous man, but the sense of history, splendour and opulence had combined to change all that. I was bricking myself. This was way beyond me. Even the fact that 'membership is by invitation only through the sponsorship of active members' implied that far better people than me were queueing up to get a game here. Good God! Even the clubs I was loaned for the occasion were, by a country mile, the best that I had ever seen, let alone used, in my life. Each wood had its own fetching hat, and each hat its own monogram. The bag that contained them had an air of quiet authority.

The locker room smelled of privilege or, more precisely, expensive cologne and the faint air of past effort well-rewarded. It was a smell that the rebel in me would like to have despised, but the rebel turned out to be nowhere as powerful as the fascinated child, and I have to say I rather liked it. Locker stared at locker over varnished slatted benches, and above a spotless floor. Golfing shoes were lined up under the benches in military precision, and a single hat hung off each hook on the front of each locker, brand competing with brand like the starting grid of a Formula one race. Little brass card holders discreetly contained the names of the owner of each locker, most of the white cards long since faded to yellow. A couple of members eased through the room on their way from the course to the bar, the words 'Merrill' and 'Lynch' dropping gently to the floor in place of 'your' and 'round, I think', which is what you tended to get from the Cabinet Maker back in West Sussex. When Mr Trump referred to 'the people that progress left behind', I rather suspect that he did not have the members of Seattle Golf Club in mind. Progress, to them, was a concept very much consigned to the rear view mirror. Progress was something that they or their families had done long ago, and they were now taking their rightful places among the rulers of the Universe.

Up to the point that we reached the first tee, it was just a case of doing as David did, and not saying anything stupid. This was a course that had hosted the Walker Cup and was regularly the venue for professional regional competitions, and it was a fair assumption that the average member could cope with those narrow fairways and speedy greens. Even though my recent implosion still hung heavy in my mind I knew that, whatever happened early on in the round, I had learned to regain some sort of control on a lost situation, and to remember what I had been taught. Never had I been so glad to have Tim's recent coaching in the memory bank. This round was about not letting David down on his home turf, much more than it was about me potentially making a dick of myself. It also helped, as it always helps, that David wanted me to enjoy the round far more than he minded how I actually performed during it.

*

It took the Rhesus Macaque Monkey decades to become adept at living in the strange, urban environment of Mumbai, decades during which the monkeys gradually learned every trick of the trade they needed to compete on equal and, ultimately, superior grounds to their human hosts. And it must be this way too for the rookie golfer suddenly finding himself in surroundings of excellence. He must learn to adapt by following a basic set of rules, handed down by word of mouth only through the mists of time.

1. Dress neutrally. Like a soldier crawling across open ground in front of an enemy gun emplacement, we must try to get through the 18 holes without ever being seen, let alone noticed, by anyone other than those we are playing with. Stopping short of pure camouflage, this hints at neutral colours and quiet tones. Nothing looks more ridiculous than someone in sharp, fluorescent diamond-patterned trousers swishing and missing in the short rough. (It is because of this that the Banker and I had given the Cabinet

Maker a pair of sharp, fluorescent diamond-patterned trousers for Christmas the previous year).

2. Read the local rules before playing. It might be as simple as knowing where a drop zone is, or as abstruse as bowing to the Lord High Trout in the pond at the 11th but, if it's there, it needs to be done.

3. Observe etiquette. Tending the flag for someone, by way of example, has the double benefit of giving you something to do, and taking your opponent's mind off the train crash of incompetence that your own clubs are responsible for. Not walking across the line of his putt helps, too.

4. Praise your opponent's good shots. Just because he is spanking the hide off you doesn't mean that he doesn't want to be appreciated for his skill. On the contrary, the warm glow that a well-placed comment can engender just might take your opponent's mind off the awfulness of your last couple of shots.

5. Minimise the gap. Each time your opponent wins a hole, which may be nearly every hole, make it look as if you are having to rack your brain to see who came out on top. 'Your hole, I think' sounds a whole lot better than 'so that's your 4 to my 9, isn't it?' As Lee Trevino once said: 'A hungry dog hunts best'. But, then again, Ron Burns said, 'you can't make anything idiot-proof because idiots are so ingenious.'

6.   Commoditise the excellent. On the same basis by which, if you give enough monkeys enough type-writers, one of them will eventually come up with the Complete Works of Shakespeare, you are almost bound to put in a few good shots. The trick when you do so is twofold: first, not to look remotely surprised, and secondly, to look vaguely disappointed that an even better outcome didn't ensue, as that had clearly been what you had been planning. As President Elect Trump made clear during his inspiring and dignified US election campaign: 'The point is, you can never be too greedy'.

7.   Judicious use of the Gimme. A sweetly-timed concession of a 3 footer, or the surprise withholding of a 12 incher, are useful weapons in the arsenal of your trying to appear more than the sum of your golfing parts. It shows that you are intellectually active, a state of affairs that might not have always been obvious to your opponents, your family, or anyone, come to think of it.

8.   Neither apologise nor swear. Ensure that the warmth of your ambient loveliness is remembered long after the revoltingness of your golf. This is something that the Cabinet Maker had got spectacularly in the wrong order over the past few months: his ambient revoltingness is remembered long after the loveliness of his golf.

9. Find grown-up things to say about the state of the world in between holes. In this way, you will create the illusion that it is probably just the extraordinary weight of your intellect and responsibilities that has got in the way of your finding enough time to master trivial sports like golf. You are, your opponent may think, too busy saving and improving the world to be expected to thrive at a leisure activity.

10. Say 'thank you'. If you forget all the others, remember this one. Being invited on to a beautiful golf course, especially when you are a novice, is a huge privilege.

Actually, you could add an 11th, if it wasn't going to spoil the agreeable symmetry of an even number. Enjoy yourself. You were not asked for your professional proximity to Rory McIlroy; you were asked because someone wanted you to have a good time. The tragedy of golf is that so many of its more frequent players forget that point, utterly, lost as they become in the angst of disappointed hope and hierarchy.

*

We can draw a veil over the next 100 or so minutes or, to be precise, the next 8.666 (recurring) holes. Let us just say that the beauty of the surroundings and the excellence of the facilities, deserved more than it got from me, and that I got full value from the holes I was playing. We talked of this and that as we went along, and I think we both

189

knew that the conversation was merely an elegant substitute for the lack of competition I was providing. All I now remember was a powerful sense of regret that the version of me who turned up at the first tee hadn't been the one who could, on his day, actually string a few decent holes together.

Everything changed, in fact, the whole course of my golfing career possibly changed, 113 yards downhill from the flag on the 9th green.

David's second shot had driven to the green unlike mine, which had come to rest hard by an irrigation tap (hence my confidence in the exact distance), well short of and below it. The bunkers defending its downhill approaches disallowed me from deploying my go-to chip-and-run 6 iron, and I had to go aerial. Classy golfers would take a pitching wedge or, at the very most, a 9 iron out of their bag to get into the middle of the green. I took an 8 iron on the basis that a good hit would put it somewhere on the green, but a really bad one would do no worse than lay it up somewhere short of the nearest bunker. Nothing going on in my brain suggested that this club selection would be any more effective than opting for any one of the other thirteen clubs in my bag, or even a table tennis bat. I simply aimed at a large bank on the left hand side of the green that would prevent an over-enthusiastic shot from scooting off deep into Upstate Washington, and swung.

There is something about being accustomed to degrees of sporting failure, rather than relative success, that makes the achievement of even the most basic aim rather thrilling. As the ball lofted up from my club in vaguely the right direction, and at vaguely the right velocity, I held the pose, club head high in the follow through, body facing the green like that David Leadbetter book told me to. Initially, my host wasn't watching, so I held the pose for a good 20 seconds longer than was strictly necessary until he was, just to ensure that I wasn't the only person who appreciated it. The ball gleamed in the sunlight as it soared over the bunker, landed roughly where it was supposed to, and then ran up towards the mown bank.

To be honest, I had stopped watching by this point, satisfied that it had done roughly what I wanted it to, so I never actually saw it roll back off the bank, curl round onto the green, and run unerringly into the hole. I couldn't have anyway, as I was way below the level of the green when I played the shot. But, whilst I wasn't watching, David was, and so were 4 members out on the putting green adjacent to the 9th Green.

'Dude, you went in,' said David, coming back down to fist-pump me in a way that would have had Peter Alliss choking on his autobiography.

'Yee-ha' shouted one of the men on the putting green. And I realised that this was the first 'yee-ha' I had ever earned in my life, other than from the Banker when he was being silly, or when he was thinking about US Treasury Bonds.

*

The rising tide lifts everything, or at least that's the theory.

For the back nine, we were joined by Jim, who had been over in Sussex with David all those months ago, and by Len, who did something significant in Seattle to do with wealth management. When you don't personally need wealth management advice there is something rather comforting in having it available, I find. After all, it was good to know that it was directly available in an emergency. All three were fine golfers who played off single figure handicaps, but all three also had kept that childish sense of competitiveness and chat that we had developed back in the UK, albeit far lower down the food chain.

No matter what one's own skill level, there is something genuinely inspiring about playing a sport alongside some-one of real proficiency. Quite apart from the muted sense of privilege that you have been allowed to share the same turf, there is so very much to appreciate in the good golfer, starting with the extraordinary sense of confidence they exude before, during and after each shot, and finishing with their calm, full-swinging, elegance. And the best of them seem more than happy to share these moments, and this skill.

In my own experience, excellence is rarely contagious; in fact, it is more likely to shine a spotlight into the yawning chasm between me and whoever I happen to be playing. But, for the next 60 or 70 minutes something extraordinary started to happen to my game, too. What I was playing was, for the first time, recognisably golf. Not just golf, but good golf. And it happened merely because David mentioned that my shots seemed to go a whole heap better if I took a full golf swing than they did if I just poked at the ball as if I wanted to surprise it. I outdrove them all on the 10th and, instead of spraying the subsequent fairway shots all over the course, my second shot, a 5 iron off the fairway, went to the edge of the green, and down in 4. Something similar happened on the 11th, albeit with one aberration in a little stand of Douglas Firs, and on the 12th, I came close to chipping in out of an adjacent bunker. I forget what happened on the 13th, but at the 525 yard 14th Par 5, I was imperious, unstoppable even.

The competition within my own head that normally raged with the progress of each round, became instead a competition to convince Len, who had never seen me play before, that I was a proper golfer. Because David and Jim hadn't had the chance to tell him how bad I was, they joined in on the conspiracy too – a game within a game. I stopped trying unfeasible shots and started to believe for the first time in my life that, if I just did what I had been told to do, it would go all right. And, as anyone who has ever played the game knows, that is when the swing becomes fuller and more natural, the balance better, and the follow through more complete. For a glorious period I was living within a virtuous circle and had reached a magical moment, a hitherto unattainable state wherein the things that I mean to happen actually were happening. I felt like the Banker sometimes looked, minus the throbbing BMW and enormous bonus cheque.

At some point, I reached a level of confidence that opened an entirely new cupboard with a whole new range of mental switches in it marked, in order, 'calm', 'serene', 'authoritative', 'cocky' and 'arrogant'. I tried the middle one of the 5 for a while before settling on 'cocky' which saw me through until I drove into a pond full of Lesser Scaup and Buffelhead (Life List of Birds numbers 1188 and 1189), whereupon I dropped back to 'Calm' for the remainder of the round. For me these were the glory hours and the only disappointment was that the Cabinet Maker wasn't there to enviously drink it all in. I texted him from the quiet of a copse I had drifted off into.

'You're history'. Only I saw later that predictive text had transmitted it as 'Your gusto', which may well have confused him.

*

The Pacific night was drawing in as we reached the 18th. The surrounding Douglas Firs melted back into a forest of dark, and the yellow lights of the clubhouse filtered out onto the final green in a welcoming way that suggested an expensive cocktail was waiting within, ready to be brought to my table by a white-jacketed, unsmiling barman called Ernesto.

Whilst I was not exactly doing the glory walk up the 18th at St Andrews, and protecting a 3 shot lead to win the Claret Jug, it was one of the first times of my life that I had finished a round with real golfers as something approaching an equal. Normally, I found, people would stare politely at me as we walked away from the last hole, with a vague sense of recognition, a memory that they had seen me somewhere before, but couldn't for the life of them put a finger on where it was. This time, I had lost, but not by much, and this entitled me to engage in post-round banter, remembering close calls below the azalea bed, chuckling at other people's drives that had failed to make it even to 200 yards. I mean, not even 200 yards, for Christ's sake! What kind of idiot couldn't get a ball that far?

It turned out that Ernesto had gone home hours ago, or had retired back in the 1930s. David showed me round the hallowed portals of the largely empty building – fragments of England that had been transplanted in the New World long before Messrs Bezos and Gates had got hold of it, and had taught us all to do things in strange, uncomfortable ways. Little square baize-topped tables sat waiting for groups of 4 imaginary people to cluster round them and start playing bridge; voluminous leather-upholstered armchairs lay in wait for golfers of my age to drop off to sleep in them, complete with broadsheet newspaper over their face. Black and white photographs of long-dead young men in baggy trousers and horn-rimmed spectacles stared out from behind dusty glass panels. Wooden panels with columns of fading gold lettering bore witness to excellence and seniority all those decades ago.

The overall effect was that of the poor old motherland that Seattle had spent decades escaping, but that only the very wealthiest could now slip back to and enjoy. Somewhere back in the deep blue yonder, we had once shown them golf, hierarchy and exclusiveness and they had adopted them as their own. And, frankly, I found I didn't give a damn that they were in charge now, not us. I had played enough golf in enough places to appreciate the light hand of tradition that lay across so many of them. This wasn't about socially ambitious individuals promoting themselves to the top of the tree; it was about respect for the generations of people who had gone before, and the importance of the standards they had established all those years ago. That isn't snobbish, or unnecessarily hierarchical, it is respectful, and durable.

Out on the balcony, a stunning view opened up over the Puget Sound, and Mount Olympus beyond. In the middle distance, coasters butted the choppy waters on their way up to Vancouver Island and container ships bearing untold cubic metres of emptiness rushed back to Ningbo or Shenzhen to collect more stuff than the western world could possibly know what to do with. Beyond it all lay a world of woods and trails, bridges and bears, ridges and mystery, and it was my world, my subversive, surprising space. 4500 miles from home, I had just played the golf of my life on one of the most beautiful courses in America, and with people I loved to be with, who defied every rotten prejudice that I had harboured about those who lived for this sport. Where I had expected its contempt, golf had treated me better than I had wanted or deserved.

All the same, I didn't belong, and I had started to know that I never would. I had been playing this game properly for over a year now – a year that had included occasional sweet highs submerged in wastelands of routine mediocrity. During that time, I had come a long way, behaviourally. I had surrendered the absurd notion that golfers were a breed apart, with their own coda of personality disorders that made them seek out discipline, etiquette, hierarchy and bright clothing, and instead had come to realise that they were just the same as the rest of us, with the same small percentage of utter tits getting the rest of them a bad name. I had come to understand that the rules and etiquette were not just there to piss off Attention-Deficit people like me, but for the utilitarian reason of giving the maximum number of people the maximum chance of having a good time. And, above all, I had discovered that of all the sports I had played in the 700 months since I myself had been the size of a golf ball, no sport more perfectly represented the compelling internal battle between what the mind wanted, and what the component muscle groups were actually able to deliver. And yet.

And yet, once again I was coming to appreciate that golf was best suited to lovers of routine and order, people like that secretary from the Cornish links course all that time ago, who measured out his life paying bills on time, and getting the best parking space outside the GP's surgery when he went to have his blood pressure checked. If the human race could be divided into two parts, I was definitely a member of the other group, that group that only sorted out their mail twice a year and had cupboards full of old jerseys with holes in that they never quite got round to chucking out. For only when there was a stable platform of routine and predictability could each shot have a chance of steadily improving. That wasn't me. I was the kind of player who invariably tried to fit one thing too many in before the game, and therefore sentenced myself to be in a hurry at the start and never quite relax enough to let my brain commit fully to the business of the round. And the driving range was another country to me, a country where they did things differently. There was more chance of Bernie Ecclestone being taller than one of his wives than there was of me practising, which meant none. And a man who never practised would never be any good.

There, on that balcony, overlooking one of the world's most magical sea approaches to a city, I realised without question that I was a guest within this game, not a resident, and that this would be a chapter of my life, not a thread that ran through it. It was a decision that I could only have reached after playing out of my skin. Any other route to it would have been fraudulent.

But we weren't finished with all this yet. Not by a long chalk.

Chapter 10

ALL FOR A SCRAP OF PAPER

Into the Land of Handicaps and Hundreds

'*The only thing standing between you and your goal is the bullshit
story you keep telling yourself as to why you can't achieve it.*'
Jordan Belfort, *Wolf of Wall Street*

The year turned, and frozen mist lay for days in amongst
the trees and fields of the valley.

The original quartet had been reunited for 36 insane
holes of Christmas golf at Goodwood between dawn and
dusk of the shortest day, and, drink by drink, scotch egg
by scotch egg, we had begun to marvel at our dawning
brilliance, as males are often inclined to. We chuckled
at the memory of our awfulness a year or so before, and
celebrated the progress we had made as if it marked us out
as chosen ones.

Over the Autumn term, the Undergraduate, had gained,
in chronological order, a beard and a brand new driver,
but the distance of his drives simply extended in inverse

proportion to his skill at the short game. Putting and chipping remained a foreign land to him, a land for dull accountants and actuaries with no grasp of the bigger picture. Golf for the Undergraduate had developed into a primal statement of manhood, and the provisional wing of his own personal development.

The rest of us, on the other hand, were just older versions of what had headed off on this journey all those months ago. The Banker was the steadiest of us, each shot played from well within his range of ability. He had been the first and only one of us to break 100 on a course, or at least a course that didn't have windmills and clowns' mouths on it. He had even persuaded his employers that he had morphed into one of those executives who could be relied on to take important customers out for adult sports days, thinly disguised as corporate hospitality. We continued to love him for his sweetness, and for the day that he would run his bank, become disgustingly rich, and look after us all.

The Cabinet Maker continued to follow the dictum that 'winners are losers who got up and gave it one more try' although, in his case, thirty more tries was nearer the mark. He had been the only one so far to get a handicap, and the first to play in a monthly medal (where his fourth place won him a third hand Goblin Teasmaid that someone wanted rid of). Jaundiced though he might be about the sport, and the people he played with, we had the sneaking impression that deep within him was a grizzled club secretary waiting to burst out and inflict himself on the Annual General Meeting. 'I think you'll find ...' he'd begin, and a room full of members would run onto the A272 to try and end it all in the evening traffic.

That left me, and even I was getting better.

We finished the round and settled down in front of the fire at the clubhouse.

'How good is all this?' asked the Banker rhetorically, waving an arm at the antique hunting prints on the wall, and the organic beers that we were nursing. We waited patiently for him to tell us how good it all was.

'It's brilliant. That's how good it is.' He was 47, slightly drunk, and going on 80. 'And we have to do it for ever'.

He had identified, as we all had, that tiny little strand of boyhood that runs into adult life, the bit that makes the awful things in life bearable. It was playtime, and we could keep doing it until the bell went. And the best thing was that the older we got, the less chance we had of actually hearing the bell when it was rung.

We were at the level of alcoholic consumption and general well-being at which the outside world starts to become something easily to be conquered, and our individual positions of importance within it easily exaggerated. The more expansively our arms waved about in animated enthusiasm, the more nervous the bar staff became about the safety of the furniture, the décor and the other members, particularly when the Undergraduate began a graphic real-time demonstration of how he had 'driven the bank' on the signature second hole. His massive club-less backswing came close to dislodging a Stubbs print off the wall, and his follow through toppled a pile of old Country Life magazines towards the fire place.

A feature of our golf over the preceding months was how much better we were at it a couple of hours before, or a couple of hours after, any given round. Shorn of equipment and pressure, we found our swings became more natural and our putting nigh on perfect.

'I'm going to give myself January to break 100 and to get a handicap,' I suddenly heard myself saying, and then in February I'm going to do a round on the best course in England. Finally, in March, I'm going back to that bloody place in Cornwall.'

The others were intrigued, especially since the histrionics of my meltdown and resignation from the sport were only a couple of short months back. The Undergraduate pointed out that, although I had played OK today, I hadn't exactly given any indication of the kind of excellence that would get me round a championship course. Being an Undergraduate, he had phrased it in slightly more robust terms than that, and there followed a faint rustle of disapproval around the room as people of quality shifted in their leather armchairs at the word he had chosen to describe his father's prowess.

It was the numbers.

Being someone who had always counted off everything all his life – paces walked, books read, birds seen, shots played – the declining numbers in terms of strokes had recently come to a standstill for me, and I needed them to move on. It had turned out that golf was the ultimate activity for someone with my affliction, since the entire thing is based on counting; but the huge improvements which had met our early efforts had dwindled to little incremental steps, punctuated by occasional plateaus and, even, troughs, as we had risen beyond a certain level. From now on, each improvement would be, almost by definition, smaller than the last, and a little bit harder to achieve. That handicap would be my numerical proof of my year's work, and the hardest course in England would simply recalibrate the existing numbers onto a new scale of competence. All those months ago we had hacked our way around the course that Tripadvisor had dared to call one of the worst in England; now it was time to go to the other end of things.

I went home and Googled 'best golf course in England'.

The Editor in Chief of 'The Top 100 courses in Britain' was unequivocal on the subject. As voted for by the kind of people who actually take the trouble to vote for these things, Royal St George's at Sandwich in Kent was in first place for the 6th year running. Others had their supporters in other lists and, further afield. People got misty eyed over Royal County Down, St Andrews and Royal Dornoch, to be sure, but it was the East Kent links[20] course that combined overall reputation with being local enough to where we lived for us to tackle it in a day. 'Imagination and creativity are likely to be called on even more than good ball striking and brute force' said one commentator. We didn't have good ball striking, brute force or creativity in our armoury, but we had imagination in bucket loads.

Royal St George's own website was even more explicit in its general description of the course: 'Demanding carries put a premium on strong driving, but even with such uncompromising terrain properly flighted and directed shots will always find their target and leave a clear line to the green.'. In a year or more of playing this game more or less seriously, we hadn't actually met a carry of more than 100 yards or so, and none of us had the faintest clue what a 'properly flighted' ball looked like. We just dared to

---

[20]Links (the word is taken from the old English for ridge) are normally undulating coastal courses where the fairways are narrow, the bunkers deep and the wind howling. They favour smug golfers who can hit low accurate shots.

believe that we were competent enough to give it a go, and good enough not to make complete idiots of ourselves.

I went into the 'Visitor' section of their website, feeling like a student walking into Harrods. I agreed to be stalked by their cookies, but hoped against hope that their cookies wouldn't report back to the Secretary that we weren't cut from the same cloth that normally booked on for a round. There was lots of terminology that was new to me: dog leg draws, accurate clubbing, two tier, turbulent greens, and a huge amount of peril. The cost was £100 for each of us, £100 being the price that I had paid for each of my first two cars. I emailed the others knowing, as I did, that what I was transmitting would be received rather differently in each of its three destinations. The Banker would see it as an opportunity for demonstrating his excellence, the Cabinet Maker as a bridgehead for his occupation of the citadels of privilege, and the Undergraduate as a terrifying invitation to spend money that he didn't have.

'Anyone up for St George's at Sandwich?' I wrote casually. 'Supposed to be most difficult in England, so may well be that one or two of you won't feel up to it.'

The threat of mindless application was temporarily enough to remind the Undergraduate that he had pressing business to attend to in academia, and the Banker that January was bonus adjudication month and it would be foolish to be absent from the office for a single second of it.

For the time being, it was just the Cabinet Maker and me.

Things didn't improve when Royal St George's sent their confirmatory email which said, amongst other things, that they were delighted we would be visiting them, and that they would respectfully like to see our handicap certificates 'of 18 or below' before they saw us. Given that I was struggling to persuade my club to give me a certificate of 28 in time for the round, and given that the Cabinet Maker was only in possession of an entirely fictional certificate from his 9 hole pitch and putt course, it looked to be something of an uphill struggle.

A significant part of the attraction of our playing a round at St George's revolved around golf's iconoclastic position in modern life. We live in a world where your cell phone can do anything for you, from telling the time to taking photographs, from downloading your emails to telling you how many calories you have expended on a particular day. However, the phone may well be able to talk to your fridge, your hot water tank, your dog food dispenser or your irrigation system, but it can't yet help you drill a ball in a straight line down a fairway. You can access any App you can imagine from Tinder to Uber and back again via Hamsterfun, but it has no answer for the un-readable putt at the 13th. And yes, you can send pictures of what you are doing on Instagram, Facebook or Pinterest, and you can tell people all about it on Facetime or Snapchat till they are sick and tired of hearing from you, but out there you are on your own. Going to somewhere like St George's seemed to represent one of the last bastions of activity in which we were left to our own devices, just us, our clubs and the dunes around us. Technology would have no part in what was to follow.

I sent off an enigmatic email to Tim, our ever helpful pro, asking him whether he could find it in his heart to send a suitable letter to St George's, at the same time as indicating that nothing was higher on my to-do list than rejoining his club for another year. Our one chance was to have a recommendation from a Professional to the effect that we were, in his opinion, capable of getting round the place without destroying it, or holding everyone up. His reply was succinct:

'I'll do what I can. Are you sure?'

*

Suddenly, golf became a serious business.

We set up a New Year four-ball with the sole aim of handing in a completed score card[21] Gone were the gimmes and most of the forgiven airshots; gone were the Portuguese

[21]Three completed scorecards are required for a handicap. Previously, ours had been too bad, or too fictional, to be valid.

caddies[22]; gone was the foolish laughter. We were here to boss the very turf beneath our feet and to go round, to really go round, in as few shots as humanly possible. In among the bullshit and bravado, there was an aching desire within us to do our stuff on one of the hardest courses in Europe, and to do so without embarrassing ourselves. That was how far we had come since the outset, since that rainy day I had stomped out of the Secretary's office and across that Cornish car park.

From tribal outsiders, we were now demanding entry into the central wigwam.

If everyone in the sixties hadn't been too busy reading *Lady Chatterley's Lover* and listening to the Tremeloes, I would probably have been diagnosed as having Attention Deficit Disorder (ADD). To the generally perplexed observer, this condition manifests itself as a lack of ability to concentrate on one thing for more than a few minutes, and on having a brain that consistently runs in a different gear to the brains around it. This might have been a useful condition to carry around in the Stone Age, where the ADD hunter heard and avoided the sabre-toothed tiger stalking round the dark camp and buggered off long before his colleagues

[22]The Portuguese Caddy. A phenomenon by which a ball that had hitherto been in an uncompromisingly awful lie in the rough suddenly appears on the edge of the fairway, easily playable. It is not known how it got its name, but apparently the Banker has ancestry from deep within the Iberian Peninsula.

had finished chewing on a juicy mammoth toe, and ended up as supper themselves. But it is death to a round of golf. Golfers, you see, operate best when they are 'in the zone', when the single thing occupying their mind is that 45 gram, 42 mm ball lying on the grass about 1.7 metres from their eyes, and what they plan to do with it. I, and others like me, see things differently. In the few seconds it has taken us to address the ball, we have already thought about the important email we forgot to send last night, the fact that the nearside front tyre on the car is a little deflated, the need to buy a new tube of toothpaste and how much something that we heard on the *Today Programme* early that morning had annoyed us. That little ball is just one of any number of things that will be demanding our attention when we swing our club through the arc, and it is a matter of chance if it is at the front of the mind at that instant when club connects with ball.

Recently, neuroscience has helped to combat the effects of this by working on an electrode cap known as an electroencephalograph, which detects restlessness in the wearer's brain, and creates subliminal signals that then persuade the brain to calm down. Originally developed for astronauts, recent work has been done with this technology on players of precision sports, most notably golfers, and the results have been impressive to say the least. An average of a 43% improvement in accuracy has been observed in blind tests, where one group had hats that did the real thing, and the other had hats that just played out a series of random bleeps. However, the fact that these tests are being carried out by very grown up Taiwanese and German scientists in laboratories, means that the technology is not yet available in Sussex golf shops, and won't be for decades to come. This in turn means that people like me continue to be hideously handicapped and therefore discriminated against. Please give generously, and thank you for listening.

In default of artificial electronic help, I was left with only my normal brain activity on this early round from 2017, but with one significant difference: this round of golf really mattered, as they all would till we had at least made our way round 18 holes of St Georges'. St Georges' would want nothing to do with us without that little scrap of paper, and it wasn't going to fall into our laps without this due process. I had to believe that even I could hold it together at a time like this. In consequence, I made myself pause before each shot and take a couple of practice swings; I tried to visualise what I wanted the ball to do, where I wanted it to go, rather than my normal habit of just trying to get it away from me as fast as I could. Back in Seattle, David had taught me the trick of starting each shot behind the ball rather than alongside it, so as to see face on what the shot was up against, and I made myself do this each time. Thus, instead of seeing the whole challenge only from the limited perspective of sideways on, and out of only one eye, you would get to see it stereoscopically, and have a much better idea of distance and depth. This was not compelling viewing for spectators and opponents, but as a tool in getting a little bit more consistent, it was invaluable.

The Undergraduate brought along his occasional employer, the Publican, and I wondered whether to pair myself with him before either of the others claimed him. He was young, tall, and had a bag that spoke of years of competence on the local courses. However, just as with cricket, where the man who inadvertently presents himself as a ringer often turns out to be as talentless as everyone else, so in golf. I suggested that we all teed off straight away so as not to cause a hold up, and then decide on the pairings as we headed off. This would give me a chance to see how good he was, and therefore how earnestly I wanted to pair up with him. In the event, his first ball sliced miles off to the right into some long grass. The Cabinet Maker and I both said a little too quickly, and in genuinely unprepared unison: 'Why don't you play with Tom?' A contemplative silence followed.

Thereafter, there were 2 games going on. The Undergraduate and the Publican were simply doing what our group had always done, thrashing their way around the course in an enjoyable way with an occasional shot of genius thrown in for good measure. The Cabinet Maker and I had, by necessity, joined the ranks of people we'd had the temerity to scorn only months before, conscious now of how much it all mattered: serious men from the community treating the game as more important than life or death. The kind of people who got round to posting all their Christmas cards by the end of the first week in December, and then insisted on telling everyone about it. On the front nine, I went round in 53, which was not bad for me but some distance from what I needed to break into double figures for the full round. But then I strung out a short purple patch after the turn with unheard of birdies at both the twelfth and the thirteenth, and followed up with one over on the next hole. Hitherto, one birdie every third round would have done me fine, but two in succession was the stuff of Bloomberg news flashes. Normal service was resumed for the next couple of holes, which left me needing to complete the eighteenth in a par score four strokes to achieve an unheard of 99.

To the traffic passing by on the road to our left, I was probably just one of four tedious looking men playing truant from work. To the members huddling around a table on the terrace whilst having a smoke, I was just someone with an ugly swing walking towards them with the faintest limp in his left leg. To my playing partners, I was a boring tosser who had gone simultaneously smug and quiet. But as far as I was concerned, I was on the fringe of greatness. I strolled down the final fairway after my drive, imagining the applause from the gallery, doffing my cap to the thousands surrounding the green and waving my putter in a manner that denoted nonchalance and calm. *Sol y sombre* is what the Spanish call this behaviour, the extreme contrast between the dark depths of shadow and the searing sunshine just the other side of the pavement, with absolutely nothing in between.

Everything depended on the next two shots.

And that's the thing about all human progress. It always ultimately hangs on what Winston Churchill called 'the hinge of fate', that precise moment when the cards either fall right for you, or fall as a complete pig's breakfast. They didn't invent the electric light by constantly improving the candle, as they say, and sometimes something completely out of the ordinary has to happen in order to move things on. If this were a romance, I would have made a complete hash of my third shot, but then miraculously pitched in from 75 yards away and got the girl after all. If it were a Gothic novel, I would have missed with both shots and then killed the attendant werewolf with a crossbow before sending its offspring to Eton by way of atonement. In a Hollywood film, it would have been as for the romance, but with the lead role played by Mel Gibson and everything that had happened in the past turning out to have been the fault of the British after all. But it was none of these things. My third shot had been completely mis-hit, and had drilled into the wooden base that surrounded the first tee, 45 degrees in the wrong direction. It then ricocheted off at a fortunate angle, and climbed miles into the air before landing on the eighteenth green, and coming to rest about 2 foot away from the flag. It was by some margin the worst shot of my round but with the sweetest of sweet outcomes. Even I wasn't going to mess up the putt from that distance.

Fact, as is so often the case, was much, much stranger than fiction.

Whether I fully deserved it or not, I finally had my sub 100 round, and I now belonged to the elite 29% of golfers, rather than the other lot. Having spent my entire sporting life in the bigger group, the 71% that can often feel that they are only there to make up the numbers, I felt I had discovered the one thing in a sporting life that was more satisfying than watching an Australian batting collapse. I walked off the green in a state of near grace.

As we approached the Pro's shop, the Cabinet Maker casually mentioned a couple of air shots that he claimed to have seen me take in the rough on the 4th, and again on the 17th, and a disputed sequence of sand shots in a bunker near the turn, and he wondered whether these had been added into the overall score. But how could he have done anything else? Inside, he must have been sobbing his heart out. If, after all the rounds in which he had beaten me hands down, if he could have chosen one particular round to stick the boot in and humiliate me, it would surely have been this one, the one where I finally had to start handing in score cards. He himself had gone round in 102 but in those three extra strokes was wrapped a whole month of bragging rights. He had never quite forgiven me for the contempt with which I had greeted his own achievement of a handicap on his school course, and I could see it had hurt him to the quick that I had just taken a giant step towards mine.

I handed my signed card to Tim who looked at it for a second or two and then smiled at me. That smile said much. It said that he knew what I had been through to get this far, and he consequently knew exactly what it meant to me. It probably also said that it would be almost impossible for me not to rejoin his club in the circumstances. The Cabinet Maker said afterwards that he thought he had seen a slight wink as well, and that this would surely indicate that I had in some way been rumbled. Tim had been the Father Confessor figure in the background of the golf I had played in the last 15 months or so, calmly insisting when asked that, if I followed the basic principles, I would make it like all the rest. People like Tim, if they're any good, enable the rest of us to have our occasional moment in the sun. They should be cherished, and occasionally fed Bounty Bars and the like.

A week later, the Cabinet Maker and I were out again in the cold light of a January dawn, but this time just the two of us. There was no connection in the next 178 minutes between what we had been doing a year ago, and what we were capable of now. 7, 6, 4, 6, 6, 5, 5, 7, 4 went my first nine holes. 5, 4, 5, 5, 7, 5, 4, 4, 6 went the next. 95

strokes to get round a course that I could hardly play 12 months ago. I had never been in a zone before that didn't have 'Congestion Charge' written in large letters in front of it, but now I was. For about 15 minutes of my life, on the fifteenth and sixteenth holes, I only took 8 shots to hit a ball 742 yards via the inside of 2 small holes no more than 108 mm wide. The last time I had felt that sort of achievement was 23 years before, when the Artist had answered 'yes' to a question that I had worried for weeks might be met with a 'no'. And, unfortunately, the Cabinet Maker matched me stroke for stroke.

We took an inexplicable selfie on the eighteenth with our ridiculous woolly hats and even more ridiculous expressions. When I look at it now, and when I cut through whatever the motives were for taking it in the first place, I see the faces of two chronically un-cool children who have just discovered the keys to the sweet cupboard. A pair of idiots, maybe, but a pair of 95s without doubt.

Literary tradition dictates that the third and final of my three qualifying rounds was filled with drama and intrigue, but it wasn't. There were the normal moments of awfulness, but rather more of routine competence. Those who have been accustomed to sporting stardom since the days their fathers took them to mini rugby on wet Sunday mornings, before they had even left primary school, or who dominated every school team until they graduated in General Brilliance (with Honours) from some Russell

Group University, would be bored by the concept of 'routine competence'. They would dismiss it as something for losers, the sort of thing that happened to them only on really bad days. But they should know, and you should all know, that routine competence is the acme of what so many of us, 71% of us four million golfers, 2.8 million people to be precise, aspire to in our sport. It is the cream on top of the tepid cappuccino of our dreams, and we are never disappointed by it. 'Bring it on!' we cry to anyone out there who will listen, long after they have all gone home for tea.

515 days after I had been shown the metaphorical door of that Cornish golf club for want of a handicap, I handed in the signed score card that would, in theory at least, permit me to go and play there[23]. Purists may murmur under their breath that not every swish out of the rough was counted, or that it was unorthodox to have the card counter-signed by someone as closely related to me as the Undergraduate,

---

[23]A further word on handicaps. Each course requires, theoretically, somewhere around 72 strokes to go round, but only if you are a scratch (ie exceptionally good) golfer. Your official handicap indicates how many strokes above that 72 you may be expected to go round in. The highest handicap a man can have is 28 (meaning 100 for the round), but we needed 24 in order to go back to Cornwall and play there, as that is the course's minimum requirement. When you play in competitions, the handicap system is supposed to even up the differences between players, and make the match interesting whatever the disparity.

but purists are just pedants with high standards, and they are easily ignored. Darkness had fallen as we made our way off the eighteenth, so the Pro's shop was closed, and the card had to be posted through the letterbox. Two or three times during that night I woke with a start and wondered if the card was OK, whether a rat might pass in the small hours and chew it up for nesting material, or an early morning cleaner might mistake it for litter, and put it in the bin. I left it for a day or two to feign indifference, and then presented myself to Tim in a nonchalant way the following Tuesday.

'How's it going?' I mumbled as I walked into his office, as if we had met by chance outside Chichester Cineworld, rather than right in the middle of his work place.

'Fine. How about you?'

I wanted him to be the one to bring the subject up, so that I could say: 'Oh that. Don't worry. Whenever you're ready. To be honest, I had forgotten all about it.'

'Fine, too.' I said.

'Was there anything else?' he asked politely. 'Did you want to book a round or something?'

'Good idea.' And I booked one, even though I had no idea whether or not I could actually play it at that time.

'Well, I'd better be getting on then,' I added. 'There was something else, if only I could remember what it was'.

But Tim knew, and he only prolonged the agony for a few more seconds before handing over a piece of paper and saying: 'Was it this, by any chance?'

When he handed the bit of paper to me, it initially struck me as looking rather inconsequential after all the months of effort and heartache it had taken me to acquire it. I think I had expected parchment at least, plus the whole thing being rolled up into one of those Medieval scrolls with red ribbon around it, for it to be handed down to me by a reigning monarch, or at least the mayor of Midhurst in his ceremonial robes. But it was not what it looked like but what it said that mattered: and what it said to anyone who could be bothered to listen, was that I could be counted on to go round a normal golf course in 96. And play more or less wherever I wanted to. Apart from Royal St Georges, where I would need the assistance of a letter from Tim. But when the time came for our round at the Royal North Cornwall, I would bring the handicap out of my pocket with a slight flourish, and lay it in front of the Secretary with a fathomless look in my eye. Having to take my cash off me would hurt him to the quick, and send him diving for the retrospective comfort of the R and A rulebook (Tournament Administrators and Referees' Conference section), and a packet of Extra Strong Mints

My Odyssey had brought me a long way. There had been many times during those eighteen months when I didn't believe that this moment would ever come; moments when I felt that the basic technique would elude me for ever, and that I would have to find something else to occupy that little space in my ambition called 'progress'. I wanted to hug him, but the Lady Captain had come into the room and was standing behind, and she might have found the action open to misinterpretation.

'Thank you, Tim', I said. And I meant it.

'You earned it,' he replied, and I think he meant it, too.

Back in my car, I let decorum and good manners reign for a good fifteen seconds before I put a call through to the Cabinet Maker at work.

'Guess what I've got?' I asked rhetorically.

'Herpes,' he said, and put the phone down on me.

Chapter 11

OF DUNES AND DUNLINS

Beyond the comfort zone, and out the other side

'*We need to internalise this idea of excellence. Not many folks try to spend a lot of time trying to be excellent.*'
Barak Obama

The small group of apes sitting high in the Baobab tree had options.

They could stay where they were in Eastern Africa, live off plants, insects, flowers or bark, and occasionally be eaten by something. Some did just that, and they stayed much as they were for many millennia to come. Or they could head east to the brackish marshes on the coastal plain, and forage for fish and crustaceans. Others did that, and the fish oil in their diet made them restless and ambitious. Then they were driven to head North to the Mediterranean, and where some turned right towards Asia, carrying with them a genetic feature on the Y chromosome known as M168. Many did that, and they ended up in Asia and Australasia, barbecuing stuff and watching marsupials and old episodes of *Neighbours*. The last group turned westwards and northwards once they got to the Mediterranean, splitting as they went, and occupying Eurasia. There, in their barrows and long huts, they quickly discovered the wheel, the art of warfare, the renaissance and the commercial airlines that could take them all the way back in 11 hours to where their journey began some 50,000 years ago. Such is progress.

My forebears did just that, and they have been complicating things for themselves ever since, which may go a tiny way towards explaining why three middle-aged men were driving through a torrential February dawn towards a golf club that was known to be about five levels above their ability, and one 21 year old was on the 6.40 a.m Southeastern service from St Pancras to Sandwich watching an episode of 'How I met your mother' on Netflix for the 30th time.

*

I had made the grave mistake of checking something on the website of the Royal St George's Golf Club just before turning in the night before. The small problem that I discovered was that we were too late by about a month to book in for the famous breakfast at the club before our round; the more significant one was that they reiterated that, under no circumstances, could the Caddy Master let us on the course without an 18 handicap certificate. Our own club could send all the fine reassurances it wanted to: without that certificate, we wouldn't even be allowed to start. Our already generous handicaps of 24 were not capable of being further bent in our favour and, besides, would count hugely against us if we ever went into competitions. This kept me awake till one in the morning, and woke me up before the alarm at 4.30, wondering what it would feel like to pay £100, drive 120 miles, and then be told that we weren't allowed on. We drove round the soaked motorway system in the contemplative silence of people who had a significant appointment with their surgeon planned. We were wondering what Plan B was, and if it might possibly entail a wildlife park with meerkats. For some reason, my family always seemed to end up looking at meerkats in wildlife parks when our plans went adrift. The rain eased up after we had collected the Undergraduate from the station, one wordless look at whom established that he had spent the night on the floor of an ex-girlfriend's house somewhere in London, and that the key of her parents' drinks cabinet had very definitely not been hidden. We left the town of Sandwich and stood outside the clubhouse taking in the setting.

Some things in life- Pork *Rilettes* and Boris Johnson for example – don't reward knowing too much about what they once were before they became what they now are. Into this category could be fairly put the manner of our booking into Royal St Georges. Things were said. Persuasive emails were sent. Claims were made, to be honest, possibly including 'alternative facts'. Money changed hands. Such was our determination to play a course of this distinction, that there was little we weren't prepared to do in is achievement. So many of the things that you most anticipate in life turn out to be anti-climaxes and, for a second on our first arrival, this looked to be one of them. The course that we had seen on the official website, picture perfect in the dawn sunlight, was not recognizable under the glowering sky; all those raised galleries and crowds watching the endless clips of the British Open we had seen on Youtube were nowhere to be seen. There was nothing inherently wrong, but it was quiet, flat and very, very empty. It had the air of a place that someone would choose to go birdwatching in, sustained by the hope that they would identify a very rare, very boring small brown thing with an annoyingly repetitive call.

In the foreground, a miserable looking Irish wolfhound sat alone in the members car park, tied up to a large golf trolley. Beyond it was the starter's hut, a place from which we had no doubt a ferocious Scottish Caddy Master would erupt as soon as we approached the first tee an hour later, demanding certificates that we hadn't earned, and didn't have. And beyond that, in the Dickensian marsh mist, loomed the folds and dunes of the course, and the faint outline of the block-like buildings of a distant commercial estate, and the invisible North Sea out in the grey yonder, where sea areas Thames and Dover meet. It was empty, desolate even, a million miles from the busy and imposing centre of excellence we had expected. A curlew called somewhere out there on the coastal margin, and I could imagine Abel Magwitch in the dunes, all leg irons and flailing hair, trying to outrun the police.

To hide his own nervousness, the Banker started to instruct the Undergraduate in how to behave in this kind of venue, an exercise as pointless as a Hilary Clinton charm offensive, given that the Undergraduate would always do what he would do, but he would do it with a measure of enthusuasm and warmth. We presented ourselves to the Professional, planning on a menu of assertiveness, charm, persuasiveness, in that order, before we threw ourselves on his mercy when all that didn't work. We were wearing collared shirts and jackets, like four air passengers hoping for an upgrade.

In an eerie echo of my visit to the Cornish golf course eighteen months ago, the Professional was needlessly straightening a small pile of score cards on the counter.

'Morning, Gents,' he said brightly after we had introduced ourselves. 'We're not busy today, so you can tee off when you like'. He handed us four score cards and pointed the way to the clubhouse. No certificate. No questions. No nothing. We duly purchased four expensive Royal St Georges' woolly hats from him, because that is the kind of thing you do when you are incredibly relieved about something, and want to show your appreciation in a way that doesn't signpost the original problem.[24]

The corridor of the empty clubhouse reeled off the roll call of excellence from the understated panelled walls: Rogers; Lyle; Norman; Curtis; Clarke, and all the others. Past Presidents with Military Crosses and Club Captains from the House of Commons vied with honours boards for tournaments and medals, and display cabinets full of ancient clubs and balls. I had spent ten minutes the previous night watching a film of Greg Norman's astonishing charge in the 1993 British Open- 13 under par, and no round over a 69. He had eaten where I was going to eat, changed into his kit where I was changing and graced the same fairways that I was going to try to play on. We exchanged glances that merely said: 'this is far, far bigger than we are'. The journey from that north Cornish car park had taken me a very long way.

After breakfast (which turned out to be mysteriously available without booking after all), and a bucket of practise balls out on the range, we headed out to the starter's hut. Aside from a few seagulls and skylarks, all

[24]One of the reasons that we almost always got onto most of the courses of our choice was that we chose to play most of our golf in the weekdays, mainly in the afternoons, when the courses were at their emptiest. Weekends were for folk in diamond-patterned sweaters to do Monthly Medals and the like. And they were much more expensive.

around was emptiness, and the blanket of quiet that a sea mist brings with it. The hut was empty, and there was no Caddy Master to be seen. All we had to do was get out of sight as quickly as we could to avoid being found out, and then to play the 6867 yard course as well as we could, and as enjoyably as we dared. And, if no one had ever told us how scary it all was, we might have made a better fist of the opening hole. But they had. And they had never stopped. And we had each spent weeks psyching ourselves up, and out, on Youtube. And emailing each other horror stories. And listening to people saying that we would never get round. And telling us that we shouldn't even be trying. And that we would need 40 spare balls to replace the ones we would lose. And that our embryonic golfing careers would be spat out on the Kent marshes as recompense for our cheek. And in consequence, our legs were like jelly. And, in one way or another, three of us clean forgot the biomechanics of the drive, shanked our opening shots sideways and then immediately turned furtively round to ensure no one had seen. Only the Undergraduate had hit a decent shot, choosing the scariest tee he had ever been on to unfurl a massive drive, straight and true, that took him almost 300 yards up the fairway.

We waited for the Cabinet Maker to say 'tosser', as was his custom, but he didn't. 'Good shot. Tom,' he said instead. That was how bad things were for us.

A fourball was approaching the first tee behind us, all

woollen hats, muffled laughter and competence, and it scared the last bit of sense out of us.

'Let's just leave our balls where they are in the rough,' I said to the Cabinet Maker and Banker. 'Let's walk 200 yards and play second shots from where they might have gone, and should have gone'. We conceded the hole to the Undergraduate and did what I had suggested, just needing to be away from expert scrutiny. But the second shots were not much better, and we walked on again. And it might have gone on this way for eighteen holes had the Cabinet Maker not paused on our walk up to the second tee and said:

'Come on. It's a golf course, not a minefield. We're here to enjoy ourselves. We've paid all this money, taken the day off, and we could waste it all. We can always call them through if it comes to it'. And that was the sanity check we needed. We realised that our brains had become obsessed with the reputation of the course, and were busy sending over-ride signals through our Central Nervous Systems telling them that everything they had learned in the last year or so was a waste of time. Not being 'found out' had become more important than playing as well as we possibly could. In this more positive mindset, we started rationalise the difficulty of the course into just two things: the omnipresence of cavernous bunkers, and the multi-layered contours of the marbled greens, each one as unreadable as a novel by Salman Rushdie. Everything else was just golf. The fairways may have been narrow, but they were the best manicured fairways we had ever seen, and our balls would roll miles if we could only find them with our tee shots. All it required was for us to do what we had already been doing every week of the year. And have a bit of luck.

And then the Cabinet Maker and I slew the first dragon we had come for.

The fourth hole at St Georges is known in the golfing community as a card-wrecker. A 494 yard Par 4[25], 80% of the hole is blind[26], which leaves you staring at the other 20%, a towering 40 foot high bunker [27]dug into a large mound about 180 yards from where you are expected to tee off. Too close to the start to contemplate laying up[28], you have no real option but to take it on. Once safely over, you are faced with a narrow fairway, more bunker, and a green that slopes in two different directions. Oh, and out-of-bounds[29] is three yards over the back. If you could compress the reason we had driven all the way over and

[25]A lot of hole in not many strokes
[26]You can't see the end from the beginning. Or even the middle, come to think of it
[27]Google it. You could fit virtually all Tony Blair's wealth inside it, and still have room for Jeremy Clarkson's ego.
[28]What scaredy cats do when they're not sure they can clear an obstacle. Play to stop just in front of it, and then have a go from closer.
[29]Where you can't go even though you can see your ball.

paid the eye watering green fee, it was that towering bunker, and that tiny feeling that we might be good enough to tame it.

On approaching it, our group's mindset had been greatly improved by being perfectly respectable on the previous two holes, and we were just starting to veer from gibbering wrecks to cocky idiots, without really ever alighting in the attractive bit called 'quietly confident' in the middle. Uniquely, in our history, the Undergraduate was 3 up after 3 holes, fuelled either by the sense of occasion or the industrial quantities of Patron Chocolate Tequila he had absorbed the night before. Or more likely, that no one had told him to be overawed, so he wasn't.

The Cabinet Maker unfurled a beautiful drive which went straight and high above the dune, in exactly the direction he had been seeking. He said nothing. I did the same, and said nothing either. For we were performing to the highest standards we knew, and then a bit, and to do so was thrilling in an uncomplicated way. Both of us were on the green in three strokes, and both putted out for a bogey[30] five. And for the next few strokes, we all went along in similar vein, chalking up between 53 and 57 strokes for the outward half of the course, and having held up no one. The Undergraduate was 1 up at the turn.[31]

---

[30]One over par. Horrible for Tiger Woods. Very heaven for us.
[31]He was slightly ahead, and being cocky.

And then on the 10th the Dragon's friend savaged the Cabinet Maker.

From his drive onwards, he seemed to develop some fatal attraction for the rough on the left side of the fairway. No matter how he tried to compensate, he kept hitting his ball further and further to the left until even Jeremy Corbyn wouldn't have wanted anything to do with it. Then, when that phase was over, he plunged into the first cavernous bunker below the green, much as Tom Kite had done on the same hole when he fell out of contention in the last round of the 1985 Open. All things are relative, though, and the Cabinet Maker would have killed for Kite's resulting triple bogey seven, having taken 3 shots alone to get out of the bunker, and finally scooted the ball right across the green to the greedy valley beyond. All square.

We all played the next hole well, missing the encircling ring of five bunkers more by luck than judgement, but then it was my turn to be eviscerated by the next Dragon. My problems started, after a decent drive, simply because I chickened out of the required lofted shot that, successfully executed, would have flown me over the ring of bunkers between me and the flag. Instead, I tried to be clever by scooting the ball along the ground in the tiny gap between two of them, and out onto the green beyond. It was a shot I did week in and week out at Southdowns and most of the other courses I had played, and it had got me out of trouble time after time. But not here. It didn't deserve to work, and it didn't. It scooted along, alright, but then it took advantage of a slight gradient to the left and rolled without apology into a sandy hole and five foot deep.

There is virtually nothing I can't tell you about the 9 bunkers protecting the 12th green because I now have personal experience of at least three of them, and had plenty of time to stare into the other six as I walked back and forward to find my ball. I learned many lessons in achieving my '11', the key one of which was, as it always is, not to try to be clever, and the subsidiary one was not to get cross. However, being mauled this way was what I had come here for, and it was no disgrace. In fact, to have gone home without displaying some of the battle scars that St Georges is famous for might even have come as something of an anti-climax.

On the 14th, a comedy hole with an out of bounds fence running its entire length about a foot and a half to the right of the tee, the Banker's sense of self-assured elegance came to the fore. Presumably spurred on by the thought that he was only a mere 45 minutes from being able to talk asset financing to his customers again, he covered the 545 yards in three shots, putting from 8 foot for a well-deserved par. The rest of us had located various thicknesses of undergrowth and dune on our way in, but we had all reached a state of mind where it was sufficient joy for just one of us to do well on each hole. The brisk coastal wind could take our lesser efforts and blow them un-noticed into the North Sea.

One of our biggest fears had been that the course would be full of Corinthian golfers, all speeding round and watching our mistakes. We had persuaded ourselves that each of our drives would take place under the curious gazes of the group behind us. As it was, the mist and rain had kept the members away, and we hardly saw anyone all morning. This suited us well, as it encouraged us to relax and not worry overmuch about what we did. The exception to the rule was the groundstaff, evidence of whose discreet attendance was on every green, in the overseeding, the sanding, the top dressing and a hundred jobs beyond. Sometimes we saw them, but, until late in the round, they were not a factor in how we played our shots.

That all changed on the short 16th, the hole made famous by Tony Jacklin achieving the first ever televised hole in one in 1967, where no less than nine of them were working on two of the seven deep bunkers that surrounded the green. As we approached the tee, 160 yards away, they laid down their tools and waited politely for us to play our drives. They would, we mused, be accustomed to excellence, and they would be expecting our balls to finish off somewhere in the middle of the green. Yet this was a hole with virtually no margin for error, and with the added problem of a strong gale blowing everything from left to right. The chances of all of us, one of us even, providing them with a shot that chimed with the standards they were entitled to expect were depressingly low, particularly as most of the pressure came from the fact that they were waiting for us to play through so that they could get on with their work.

To no one's surprise, the Banker laid up, and to even less people's surprise, the Undergraduate overshot. The Cabinet Maker stepped up, having selected a hybrid, theoretically at least, to keep the ball below the worst of the wind and chance his arm with clearing the four monster sand traps guarding the front of the hole. In the event, he hit it very slightly high, but perfectly straight and to within about 20 foot of the pin. It was as good as he could possibly have aspired to.

'No pressure, then,' he added helpfully.

But he was right, even if it wasn't what he had meant. There *was* no pressure. For this whole day was a joint endeavour, within which the role of our personal competition hardly even merited a walk-on part. We were here to get round this fabled golf course in as good order as we possibly could, and who won between the four of us had nothing to do with it[32]. By landing his ball in the perfect place, he had announced to the watching ground

[32]According to the Undergraduate, it now does matter, apparently. He would like the world to know that he won the match by 5 shots. He also took 8 on the 18th, where I seem to remember that I needed only 5.

staff that, whatever happened to my ball, we were proper golfers, and they didn't have to worry.

I pulled the driver out of my bag.[33] I had decided that I might as well be hung for a sheep as for a lamb, and nothing would look more pathetic to the waiting ground staff than my scuffing it timidly down the bank and into one of the bunkers. So I deliberately planned a colossal over-hit to the area of dunes 50 yards behind the green where the Undergraduate found himself, figuring out that I could repair the damage in privacy, rather than in the public gaze. It didn't really occur to me at that stage to go for the green.

'Interesting choice,' said the Banker, and 18 eyes strained up the hillside to see what would happen next.

'The truth, as Jessica Lynch said, is always more heroic than the hype', and I have to say that what happened next was rather awesome. As I reached the zenith of my backswing, I had a 'sod it' moment, a seminal 'sod it' moment, even. My golf was worth more than the second best that clouting my ball into the dunes would give me. At my best, I could play this game, and play it OK. It was time to stop playing the incompetence card, and prove to

---

[33] An unusually powerful club for a short hole. Real golfers would scratch their head at this choice, although the Cabinet Maker is not a real golfer.

myself that what I had only dreamed of in that Cornish car park was what I really could now do. I had served a patient apprenticeship, and why the hell shouldn't I go directly for the heart of green? So what if it was surrounded by bunkers like pearls on the string of a necklace? It may well go wrong. It probably would go wrong. But how much better to plough heroically off into 6 foot of sand than to die wondering?

So, instead of giving the ball everything I had got, I gave it plenty of time, and then a measured half swing. As I played it, I stared down at the tee and refused to lift my eyes, in case in doing so I lifted my head and top-edged the ball. A golfer can tell if the shot is a good one long before he sees the trajectory of the ball, just by the sweetness and sound of the contact, and I knew instantly it would be fine. For about five seconds, I thought it would be much better than fine, and for about a second and a half, it occurred to me that it might, just might, go straight in. The upwind line was perfect, the distance looked pretty good, too, and it had got enough elevation for me to know that it wouldn't roll far. Eventually, it landed just to the front and right of the pin, and then rolled about a dozen feet off to another part of the green. It wouldn't be a birdie, but it might just be a par. We saluted our achievements with a quick group high-five, muted because the last thing we wanted was for our audience to think that we were remotely pleased with our tee shots. And, anyway, whatever the ground staff may have thought of our shots, however shaky our putting, I had just taken a giant step towards slaying the biggest dragon of them all, my own expectations of myself.

'Shame,' I said in a stage whisper as we approached the Cabinet Maker's ball. 'I really thought you had something there. Maybe just a bit more follow through.'

Somewhere in the nineteen sixties, the western world decided that it had had enough of excellence, and that it wanted all its citizens to dwell in an unchallenging grey band somewhere between slightly grim and acceptable. I'm not sure what the point of it was, but the effect was that the concept of elitism went almost overnight from being a compliment to being an insult. Anything good was to be resented unless everyone was allowed to do it, and be good at it. Progressive schools jettisoned competitive sports in case any of the little darlings who were useless at games got offended by their own lack of achievement. But, and I speak as one of those former useless little darlings myself, what we were doing today was elite, exclusive and selective, and so much better for that. We had scraped into the club by the skin of our teeth, and going round it was life-enhancingly exhilarating.

In the end, it was the Undergraduate who prevailed. Hopelessly out of practice, wearing the most marginally acceptable of kit and nursing a weapons-grade hangover, he managed to start well, and finish well, and that was enough. The man who was so far off a handicap that he didn't even bother to ask for one, and who had had to beg Tim the Southdowns Professional for a flattering letter of recommendation, had gone round one of the hardest courses in Europe in 102[34]. For the demons of ambition had not tapped him on the shoulder, or, if they had, he was too relaxed to have noticed. He had hardly played since Bondi Beach four months before, but he had out-performed all of us.

Aside from the first hole, we had been honest with the scoring and, when we reviewed the card later on, we realized with some surprise that we had performed much the best on the four most difficult holes, those with the lowest stroke indexes, whereas the 'easier' holes tended to have overpowered us. The Cabinet Maker put it down to a weird combination of effort and focus applied at exactly the right time and place whereas the truth was probably rather more prosaic: so long as you kept out of trouble, whatever the hole, you would be OK. But the genius of Royal St Georges is that, once you find that trouble, only the very best golfers can deal with it effectively.

*

[34]A score that would have any professional weeping, and would be almost unthinkably bad for most weekend golfers at their own clubs, seemed to us almost unthinkably good. We had stood on the first tee and agreed that 125 would be perfectly acceptable.

Near the end of our round, we met a group of cheerful touring golfers from the Royal Birkdale. We agreed to have a pint together in the Smoking Room (there is no bar, as such) if we were all still around once they had finished their second round. For our part, we felt some of their excellence would rub off on us, and they, in turn, liked the sense of reckless optimism that had driven us to the course in the first place.

'Make sure you have the lunch,' one of them said. 'Truly excellent'

We explained that we couldn't go into the dining room as we hadn't brought along ties.

'Oh that's OK,' said the first. 'You'll find a load of blue and red ties with a small logo on them, hanging over our jackets in the locker room. Borrow them. There can't be that many ties in there.'

It was a kind gesture, much in keeping with the vast majority of attitudes we had come across during the time we had been playing. However, when we went into the locker room to scrub up, change and prepare for lunch, different blue and red ties seemed to have bloomed all over the place. It was as if all of golf had chosen red and blue as mandatory colours for a club tie, and we had to choose one that looked as though it might have come from a golf club we knew nothing of. Get this wrong, and it was theft, not an easy thing to explain when we were being shepherded out to the car park. We became aware of a couple of CCTV cameras covering the locker room, a development that simultaneously made the Cabinet Maker go ridiculously furtive, as if he was about to commit a capital offence, and made me do the exact opposite, staring boldly into the camera and I assertively tried on ties and challenged the watcher to see anything wrong in it. Guilt from the course had simply mutated to guilt in the clubhouse.

The British class system reveals itself in many guises, most of them utterly counter-productive. But there are exceptions, and one of these is when it does so gastronomically, as it did with the Royal St Georges' roast dinner. For there is a section of the British upper class that understand and celebrate comfort food at a level of competent simplicity that Heston Blumenthal just couldn't aspire to. Like the Alpine Swift that returns instinctively to where it was born after a flight of some 4000 miles, men of a certain stamp return unerringly to a particular kind of trough. They crave what Nanny once gave them, and what Nanny gave them was roast potatoes, rich gravy, cauliflower cheese in abundance, and lashings of rice pudding, treacle tart and the queen of puddings. Molecular Chefs may well present a signature dish of deconstructed bread and butter pudding with a frangipan and mozzarella jus (£45.00), but your average Henry, who let's face it took 129 years to allow women to join his club, just wants to get his teeth into good old stodge. And, if only in this respect, I may be marked down as your average Henry. The golf we had been allowed to play was treat enough, but to ingest 1200 calories of this kind of lunch raised it to yet another level.

It was late by the time we started our lunch, and consequently there was just the four of us in a dining room that could easily have accommodated 100. As we ate, we began to realize that now was the time to claim our prize, and to return to the monosyllabic Club Secretary 320 miles away from us in Cornwall. We had served the apprenticeship over the last eighteen months, and we had paid our dues. If we could get round the most tricky golf course in England without making complete tits of ourselves, we could probably scrape round the one where the adventure had all started. Now was the time for the four of us to bang our handicap certificates on his neatly polished counter, look him in the eye and demand that he take our money. That would teach him.

Towards the end of the meal, the Banker and the Undergraduate went off to drink in the heritage in the corridors and rooms around us. The Cabinet Maker and I became reflective. We were on the same social level in what we did, the way we thought and how we lived our lives. However, my family had been dukes only 120 years before, since when our trajectory had been firmly downwards, whilst the Cabinet Maker's had been farm labourers, and they were very much on the way up. We thanked the God of Coincidences that had enabled us to meet in the middle and establish a friendship that, in turn, could marvel in childlike clarity at the sheer fortune that allowed us to have days out like this. The Australians call it 'mateship'. Back all those years ago, the second Duke might have been able to ride from Buckingham to London and never leave his land, he might have had one of the grandest houses in all England, and he might have had 144 pipes of port in his cellar; but he didn't have this. He couldn't just call up a friend, say 'fuck it', and do something really childish.

'Enjoy it,' said the Cabinet Maker from the deep leather arm chair in the Smoking Room, draining his small cup of over-brewed coffee. 'Because in a couple of generations we won't even be talking to you.'

The staccato sound of a breathless snore came from deep within another of the leather arm chairs across the room, and we tiptoed out to return our borrowed ties back to their owners' lockers, and ourselves back to reality.

Chapter 12

JOURNEY'S END

Conjuring tricks on the Cornish Riviera

'Criticism is prejudice made plausible'
HL Mencken

In hindsight, I may have built it all up a bit strongly.

My promise to the herring gulls those two Autumns before had become a *cause celebre* and not just for me; it had dragged in a full supporting cast, and had pumped thousands more pounds into the already bloated $70 billion golf industry. It had taken me from Southfield to Sydney and back again to Sussex via Seattle. I had played some 1044 holes of golf on 19 courses in seven counties, four countries and three continents, plumbing the depths, to be sure, but also touching the occasional high. I had jeopardised not one, but three marriages, and kept a promising Undergraduate from his Business Studies far, far more than a father should. I had dragged a total of around thirty friends and relatives round golf courses in the name of research, and, depending on whether one follows the Arithmetic or Geometric Mean, had caused to be subtracted from the stocks of the brewing industry some 1392 pints of lager and about half that of bitter. During that time, I had perhaps developed from a C minus golfer to, at my best, a B minus one, and had extended my repertoire from using just 5 of my own clubs to pretty much all 14.

By the end of it all, I had surrendered at least four deep-seated prejudices at the same time as absorbing a couple of new ones. And I had met and been formally introduced to an Estuarine Crocodile.

'Life is a pilgrimage,' said Swami Sivananda, though possibly not about golf. 'The wise man does not rest by roadside inns. He marches direct to the illimitable domain of eternal bliss, his ultimate destination'. He would have been proud enough that we had located eternal bliss, as it happens, but disappointed by the fact that most of it happened to be found inside those roadside inns, and long after we had stopped marching.

Things were complicated by the fact that, of the four of us, only the Cabinet Maker and I had handicaps. This had worked at Royal St George's, where a letter of recommendation from Tim the Professional had squared things, but a quick call to Royal North Cornwall a few days earlier to check that the same procedure would work had been met with a stern refusal. 'Handicap certificates will be required,' said an unbending voice at the other end of the line, a voice that may or may not have been my nemesis from eighteen months before. On the one hand this was wonderful news, as it proved to my colleagues that the place was as grim as I had been describing, and it gave the whole enterprise the feeling of a military campaign; on the other hand, it was their club not ours, and a refusal could not lead to anything other than the four of us leaving with our tails between our legs. The situation was solved, temporarily at least, by the arrival of a mysterious email from the Banker a couple of days before we were due down there:

'I am no longer a Banker. I am an Insurance Broker called Ian, and I play off 17 at West Derby Golf Club, near Liverpool. Tom is no longer an Undergraduate. He is a Derivatives Salesman called Darren, and he plays off 22 at the Bristol and Clifton Golf Club. Just don't ask either of us to pay by credit or debit card'.

'Explain,' I emailed back, and he explained. From now on, we meant business, and our quartet had entered the realms of identity fraud.

There was allegorical talk between us on the way down the A30 in the Banker's masterpiece of German engineering. This was the French Revolution writ in golf. The secretary at Royal North Cornwall was Marat and we four collectively were Charlotte Corday, come to metaphorically stab him in his bath[35]. In addition, The Banker was Napoleon, supervising our campaign and looking just a little too imperial for our liking; the Cabinet Maker was some annoying Girondist revolutionary, and the Undergraduate was some grubby urchin eating a fellow crew member on Gericault's *Raft of the Medusa*. It all made so much sense. As for me, I was the painter Jacques-Louis David, faithfully recording every step of the way for posterity.

To ensure that we were as good as we could possibly be on the day, we had arrived the previous morning, and got in 18 holes at a comparable links course in the same vicinity as the Royal North Cornwall. It went nicely[36], and would have augured well for the following day had not we reprised the match by playing 18 'holes' of Penang Rummy in our hotel bar later that evening and run up a bill that even had the bar manager scratching his head and checking it to see if he had got it right. Whilst not necessarily being subdued the next morning, we were a little jaded, and felt on reflection that we had allowed a lack of judgement to get in the way of our preparations for the important battle ahead.

[35]This might seem a curious end for a revolutionary, but Marat was bound to be stabbed in his bath, as he spent twelve hours a day in it. Just saying.
[36]I won by 2 strokes, hence why it went nicely. As far as the other three were concerned, it was probably something of a disappointment, albeit one I can just about live with.

The car park at the Royal North Cornwall, it seemed, had a nominated space for everyone in the Western Hemisphere apart from us. Whoever you were, so long as you weren't us, you had a designated place to put your car: the president, captain, lady captain, past captains, treasurer, past presidents, groundsman, barman, professional, the village butcher and even one for the small boring person with a clipped moustache who had a Masters in simply being irritated by human progress. I hadn't noticed this the previous time I was here, and was happy to be able to point out to the rest of my team that this was further proof that what I had been telling them had been right all along, that the place oozed unreasonable authority and hierarchy in equal measure. The Banker, who had been aiming for a nominated car parking space throughout his entire career, said nothing.

Whilst the rest of us had turned up more or less ready to play, with only the shoes to change, the 'Derivatives Salesman' had headed off to the locker room with a large overnight bag to sort himself out. What went in there at 9.22 a.m had little or nothing to do with what came out six minutes later. Gone was the traditional garb of the traditional moth-eaten Undergraduate, and in its place emerged, like a butterfly from a chrysalis, something more or less completely transformed. He had taken all too literally our exhortations not to 'let the side down' by being scruffy, and had borrowed the entire ensemble from a friend of a friend at University, who had received sponsored kit by playing for his County. The matching blue trousers and shirt were from the Hugo Boss collection (designed for Henrik Stenson) and the whole thing was topped off by a Ralph Lauren Bi-swing navy windbreaker and a Bryson Dechambeau cap (2015 model). The overall £500 price tag could comfortably have encompassed everything that the other three of us were wearing, and and would still have left enough money for two tanks of petrol and a car full of Malcolm Barnecutte's excellent Cornish pasties for the way back. With a new name, new identity, new kit and a new attitude, the only thing that prevented this being another example of the paradox of Theseus' ship was the presence at his side his original £149.00 full set of promotional golf clubs. And the complete absence of a short game. And the beard. His buddy may well have lent him the clothes, including the Bionic Stable-Grip glove, but he clearly wasn't letting his clubs out of his sight.

'Tosser,' said the Cabinet Maker, but the Banker, who loved all brands almost as much as he loved designated parking spaces , was lost in admiration.

The tee-off had been booked for 10.10, and so at 9.45 we climbed the steps to the clubhouse and presented ourselves at the reception desk. We felt like we were extras in that bit in the *Great Escape* where Richard Attenborough and Gordon Jackson are first intercepted by the Nazi agent whilst boarding the bus to Switzerland. The receptionist was on the phone, but soon finished the call and apologised for keeping us waiting.

'What a lovely day you've picked for it,' he said as he took my debit card. 'It's playing beautifully at the moment.'

The 'Insurance Broker' put his handicap certificate on the desk only to be told: 'Oh, don't worry about that. Just go out and enjoy yourselves out there. You've even got time for some practise balls on the range.' As we scuttled back out into the sunshine, he added:

'Try to aim for the front of the greens if you can. They're about as fast as they can get at the moment'.

He was possibly the nicest person we had met in eighteen months of golf and, to be honest, it felt like a bit of a betrayal.

*

If Shakespeare had been a golfer, he would have found a phrase for that thrill of anticipation engendered by standing on the first tee of a new, beautiful and challenging golf course, on a sunny day with the sea glittering in the distance and the gulls screaming in the air above. But he wasn't, so we had to make do with the Cabinet Maker's poetry instead;

'Blimey! That's awesome'. He was right; it was, and for a

moment we paused to drink it all in. As he had said all those months ago in London, so he repeated here. 'We're so lucky, you know. Just to be here with our mates, let alone play.' We knew what he meant. Modern lives tend to be swamped by the order and routine necessary to just keep ones' head above water in the workplace, or in the schoolyard. There is so much that *has* to be done on a daily or weekly basis, and the joy of what we were doing right now was that it came under the category of what *can* be done. Because 'has' is conditional, 'can' is so potentially joyful.

I explained how I felt now that I was back where I had started, finally playing on those alluring folds and dunes that I had been denied the previous time that I had showed up. I could have done it all in an easier way; I could in all probability turned up the next day and just told them I had a handicap certificate but had left it at home accidentally, and they would have let me on. But to have done so would have denied the four of us the pilgrimage that had led us here, and the joy that it entailed.

If the story of our round at Royal St George's the previous month had been about the Undergraduate's raw power and lack of reasonable fear, our day at Royal North Cornwall was about the Cabinet Maker's astonishing powers of recovery.

He began the round horribly, with all the coordination

of a Dalek trying to climb a staircase. Perhaps it was the unfeasible volume of gin he had gone through the night before, or maybe it was just that the occasion had finally got to him, but he had started his campaign with 36 strokes to complete the first four holes (which happened to be one more than the card allowed for the whole of the first nine). From the moment of his opening drive, he seemed to be determined to visit as many parts of the course as he could, and to extract as much value out of his green fee as time permitted him to. It was as if he was following a guide to the flora and fauna of North Cornwall that required him to criss-cross the fairway at frequent intervals so as not to miss the nesting place of a Cornish Chough, or locate some rare Pyramidal Orchid.

During this part of the day, we only saw him rarely, like a miasma that was drifting first one way and then the other, across a belt of industrial marshland. It was a state of affairs that suited us well given the grump he was falling into. It was not that we didn't feel for him- after all, something that he had been looking forward to for months was crumbling in his hands- it was just that he was starting to spoil our morning.

Then things started to change for him at the 6th, which is something of a signature hole, and he proceeded to unleash some extraordinary golf over the next seven. On the most difficult course we had ever played, one that in our opinion made Royal St Georges' seem almost easy, he knocked off three pars in succession, and bogeyed the other four[37]. No obstacle seemed to get in his way, and each risk that he took ended up working for him even better than the last one. We felt that he was as close to being elegant as a man can possibly get whilst still looking uncannily like President Francois Hollande[38]. Taking into account the stroke indexes, it was the equivalent of playing to a handicap of about nine, and there is no golf club on earth that wouldn't welcome someone in who could do that. You had to like him very much indeed not to feel the need to wrap a nine iron around that smug expression each time he retrieved his ball from the hole, and sadly we did.

Things were changing in other ways, too.

On the tenth, one of the most challenging holes in the sport and with no margin for error, I had driven 250 yards pinpoint straight and threaded my little ball to within 190 yards of the green, no mean feat when my game has all the fissile potential to explode as a World War 2 torpedo, when it is under pressure. The Banker had already put two balls

[37] For the benefit of non-golfers, this is really high quality stuff, with roughly the same chance of happening as there is of Prince Charles saying: 'Oh, I don't really have an opinion on that'

[38] The Cabinet Maker was once given a free meal during our French cricket tour simply because he had the good fortune to be a *doppelganger* for Hollande in the only socialist restaurant left in France. Or anywhere else, come to think of it.

out of bounds, and was attending my next shot with the special interest of a man who dearly wanted it to go very wrong indeed. I didn't disappoint. I took out my hybrid with the comic notion that I could overfly wood, stream, pathway, bunker and bog and then miraculously land in the middle of the green and not roll at all. The chances of it coming off were relatively close to zero, like Stephen Fry's chances of coming over as sincere at an awards ceremony. The only thing that matched my cockiness was my titanic backswing, and the Banker's expression when it ended in an air shot. Now, to a large extent, we had reached a level of competence where air shots were a thing of the past but, on the rare occasions they did happen, we tended to be prepared to forgive them as 'practise swings', and not count them towards the score as rules dictate. Not today we didn't. Not according to the Banker.

'That's two,' he said, with the unwavering stare of an Asset Finance Manager who had just re-possessed a printing machine from un unreliable client. 'Take your time.'

I opened my mouth to suggest that he wasn't being serious, particularly when it looked as though the Undergraduate was going to speak up for me, but then we both thought better of it. He was right. There had to come a point in our journey when we played by *all* the rules, and not just the ones that suited us. Not to do so was not just disrespectful to the game of golf, but to all the hard yards we had put in to getting better at it. I accepted the decision gracefully and lofted my third shot gently into the holding area to the right of the green where pussies laid up to avoid trouble.

'What's happened to you? You never even argued.' He put his right arm over my shoulder and offered me a little nip of Laphroig[39] for my good behaviour.

*

The only thing we did completely wrong at both of the Cornish links courses we played on was to call the group behind through.[40]

Quite apart from the complete absence of anything resembling the word 'thank you' as they moved past us, they then held us up for nearly 15 minutes whilst they ponced around on the eleventh green, theatrically measuring out the distance of each of their balls from the pin, and taking as long as they possibly could over completing the hole. Whilst this didn't really worry me, as it gave me a chance to take in the view of the estuary

[39]Rocket fuel from the Isle of Islay designed to reconnect a man and his taste buds after they have been savagely separated the previous evening.

[40]It is considered polite to 'call through' a faster group of golfers behind, so as not to hold them up. It nearly always ends up in being held up by the very people you have called through, who suddenly slow everything up having got what they wanted, whilst simultaneously annoying the genuinely faster group who were behind them in the first place.

and identify a little brown bird[41] in a neighbouring thicket, it got right amongst the Cabinet Maker and the Undergraduate to an extraordinary degree, who promptly threw in a 13 and a 12 respectively at the thirteenth. My going down for a par four at the same hole meant that the seemingly impregnable eight stroke advantage that the former had enjoyed just minutes before, had evaporated in the early Spring sunshine and become a one shot deficit. For a while, I was alone at the top of the leader-board, but only for a while.

Every level of sport works if a certain competitive formula is adhered to. All participants must try their hardest to win, consistent with playing by the rules, not playing mind games and not being a tit when it all goes wrong. At our level, it was statistically unlikely that one player could get an unassailable lead by holding it together for more than half an hour, or that another could fall from grace so completely that they would have become eligible for a job in Jeremy Corbyn's shadow cabinet.

And so we wound our way round the last five holes of our journey, marvelling at the vista that each hole presented, and the fiendish cunning of the person who had designed

---

[41]It was a Goldcrest (*regulus regulus*). I offer this on the offchance that someone out there may be more interested than my three playing partners, who told me in effect that they had lost count of the number of fucks they couldn't give about me and my bloody birds, and that I was the most boring man they had ever met.

them over 100 years ago. We all had our moments, but the course always seemed to have the last laugh, rolling our balls out of bounds when we felt we had driven perfectly straight, and endlessly taunting our soft putts with overshoots on the marbled, rapier quick greens. Whilst the Royal North Cornwall didn't exactly chew us up and spit us out as we had feared it might, it proved beyond all reasonable doubt that the Secretary knew what he was talking about when he had said that I couldn't play there without a handicap. We were just about good enough to be there, and it had taken all the previous 1000 holes of golf to get us to that point. Having managed to lose only one ball at Royal St Georges, and one on the links the day before, I had lost eight by the time I had finished here, and had found none to replace them.

The Cabinet Maker carried a five shot lead over the Banker and I onto the eighteenth hole, with the Undergraduate a few shots behind us and, despite shanking his drive into the protected vegetation of the adjacent dunes, he had enough of a lead to take the day. We shook hands on the final green, and realised how privileged we had been to spend five hours here, in the sunshine, and in each other's company.

'Beers are on me,' said the Undergraduate, and for once he had remembered his wallet.

*

There was a strange sense of nostalgia hovering over our lunch in the clubhouse, like the last day of a holiday just before the cases have to be packed for the long journey home. Having been aiming for this day for well over a year, we had reached a logical full stop in the adventure, and now had to decide afresh which direction it would take. It had never occurred to me that the reward would be more in the journey than the destination and, now that we had arrived, a degree of the inbuilt innocence had disappeared. Each of us had to go back to their own real world now and recalibrate.

The Undergraduate went up to the bar and duly bought the beers from a smiling barman. From a distance and from behind, he looked like a real golfer in his new kit, like someone who might just have been shepherding some elderly friends of his parents around his local course. Which, in some ways, he had. He certainly didn't look like what he was, and what we all were, chancers from a couple of hundred miles east who had struggled to get round in less than 20 strokes over what was permitted by their handicaps.[42] If he had learned anything, it was the concept of progress through patience. That and how to blast a small white spherical thing the length of three football pitches.

The Banker leant back in his chair and watched an elderly

[42]Work it out for yourself.

four-ball, all craft and minimal effort, arriving on the final green, as they probably had every Friday these last twenty years. He had brought grace and poise to our quartet, the one member of it who could be relied upon never to sink so low that his presence became an embarrassment, but never to rise so high that we started to hate him. He had started the year by pulling his phone out of his trouser pocket at the outset of virtually every hole, so as to keep in close touch with the illusory world of finance. By the end, he was able to ignore it to the point that there were 358 unanswered messages for him at the conclusion of our Cornwall adventure. 'They'll still be there tomorrow when I go back to the office,' he said, stuffing the phone back in his pocket.

As for me, it had been my *Ballad of Lucy Jordan* moment, only without the breasts, the embarrassing rooftop climb and the hallucinogenic drugs. Golf had tapped me on the shoulder, frankly, at a time when I needed something to remind me I could still start something new, and amount to something different. My job had changed, and my children had gone from being dependent schoolboys to being largely absent young men in the time it took to say 'Student loan'. I had started by thinking the sport slightly comic, wrapped up as it was in all its laughable rules and etiquette and had ended by being mesmerised by it. I had seen myself as somehow above it, a commentator elevated from the action, and immune from its pretensions. It had simply never occurred to me when I had originally stomped away from the North Cornwall car park that I would end up by loving and needing it, albeit sometimes in a Stockholm Syndrome manner.

My phone silently buzzed the arrival of a text message, and I looked down furtively so as not to break any club rules. It was The Artist:

'Was it fun in the end?' she asked.

*

Lunch arrived, brought to us by yet another irrepressibly cheerful staff member, who wanted to know how we had found ourselves at the Royal North Cornwall, and whether we had enjoyed our day. Eighteen months of my telling the world that this place was some sort of *gulag* were starting to wear a little thin. The Banker and the Undergraduate engaged her in animated conversation, telling her the story of how we had come to be there, and promising that we would be back year after year until we were too old to drag our bags up a sand dune, and too incontinent to get all the way to the ninth green without a toilet break. My attention drifted around the room, partly absorbed by the others around us, and partly interested in where the Cabinet Maker had disappeared to a full fifteen minutes before.

When I finally spotted him, it was like waking up 220 pages in to a Kafka novel. He was standing at the bar talking to the very man who had told me that I could keep my money, and not to bother to come back until I had a handicap certificate, the man I still took to be the Secretary. For a second, I assumed that he was telling him the whole story, remonstrating at the same time as inviting him to apologise for the injustice that had been done to me. However, the body language suggested otherwise. The body language suggested that these were two peas in a pod, and that both had found a soul mate to share things with in a difficult world. There was a bit of expansive arm waving from the Cabinet Maker and then roars of laughter from the Secretary. I wandered over to a nearby notice board so that I could pretend to read about signing up for a monthly medal whilst straining my ears to hear what they were talking about.

'I think you'll find ...' I heard the Cabinet Maker saying, and knew instinctively that my place was elsewhere. If he was saying 'I think you'll find' at this early stage of a relationship, the writing was on the wall, and he was already in it up to his neck.

In a parody of the closing moments of *Animal Farm*, when the farm animals stare through the window from pig to man, and back again, and are unable to work out which was which, the Cabinet Maker was slowly metamorphosing into a Golf Club Secretary.

It was time to return him back to his people.